Discovering Derbyshire

Discovering Derbyshire

by
'Spartina'
revised by Daphne Tibbitt

Dalesman Books
1981

The Dalesman Publishing Company Ltd.,
Clapham, via Lancaster, LA2 8EB.

First published 1975
(as 'Derbyshire: A Visitor's Guide')

This edition 1981
© 'Spartina' 1975, Daphne Tibbitt 1981

ISBN: 0 85206 642 2

In preparing this guide the author would like to thank all those persons who have so willingly supplied information and without whose help this book would not have been possible, including The Arkwright Society; British Tourist Board; Cromford Canal Society Ltd; Department of Archaeology, Manchester University; Midland Railway ·Trust Ltd; The National Trust; Peak District Mines Historical Society and the Peak Park Joint Planning Board.

Printed by Galava Printing Company Limited, Nelson, Lancashire.

Contents

Cover drawing by J.J. Thomlinson. Back cover map and drawing on page 24 by C.H. Jackson. Map on page 6 by A.F.G. Stanham. All other drawings by Audrey Hopkins.

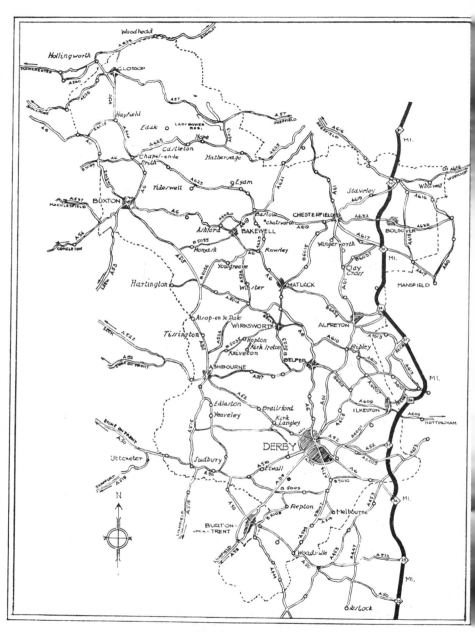

Introduction

THE county of Derbyshire holds within its boundaries a great variety of scenes, moods and memories. As you drive along the grey ribbon of a twentieth century road you may be within yards of where sabre-tooth tigers once stalked their prey in prehistoric times. Much later the Romans left their mark upon the countryside, mining for lead in the Wirksworth area and taking the mineral waters at Aquae Arnemetiae, or Buxton as it is now called. Nearer to our own time we can trace the fortunes of Bess of Hardwick, that remarkably enterprising sixteenth century lady whose memory lives on in the stones of Hardwick Hall, Chatsworth and Wingfield Manor. With the beginning of industrialisation Derbyshire gradually moved forward, with such names as Richard Arkwright and William Duesbury leading the way. Today, Derbyshire maintains its unique character combining natural beauty and the works of man, ancient customs and modern progress; and visitors are certain to find something that appeals to their particular interest. We hope that this book will help them in their search.

Throughout the guide, unless otherwise stated, admission charges are made.

1. Castles and Halls

BOLSOVER CASTLE
Route: South of A632 Bolsover — Chesterfield Road. Department of Environment. Car Parking. Opening:- daily at 9 am, also Sundays April to September, other Sundays open at 2 pm. Closing time 5.30 pm March, April and October; 7 pm May to September inclusive; 4 pm November to February.

The first recorded building on this site appears in the Domesday Book, at which time the land belonged to William Peverel (or Peveril) whose name was also linked with Peveril Castle and Haddon Hall. As the natural son of William the Conqueror it is not perhaps surprising he should have been granted so much land in the area. Nothing now remains of the original structure, but it must have been a fortress impressive enough to arouse Henry II's interest because he took over the castle in 1155. As Crown Land it later passed to Henry VII and in 1514 was bestowed by Henry VIII upon the Howard family, Dukes of Norfolk. By 1553 it had passed to the Talbot family.

Sir Charles Cavendish, son of Bess of Hardwick, bought the property in 1613 and engaged Robert Smythson to design a house in keeping with the Norman ruins upon which it was to stand. Although built in medieval style, of local red sandstone, the interior furnishing was Jacobean; it is portions of this building which remain today. Additions by 1629 had included the Long Gallery in which Charles 1st and Queen Henrietta Maria were provided with a 'stupendous entertainment' for which Ben Johnson wrote the masque 'Love's Welcome'.

During the Civil War the castle was reduced to ruins. Restoration was carried out during the 1660s by William, 1st Duke of Newcastle (son of Sir Charles Cavendish), who also built the Riding School. Visitors can see a 500 foot section of the bailey wall which encloses the courtyard of the 'Little Castle', standing four storeys high and containing 26 rooms, most of which have vaulted ceilings, ornate panelling and notable fireplaces.

8

CASTLETON: PEVERIL CASTLE

Route: South of the A625 Sheffield — Macclesfield road. Department of the Environment. Opening times:- Open daily 9.30; also on Sundays April to October inclusive from 2 pm.

Peveril Castle stands on top of Castle Hill overlooking the town and in Norman times must have had an almost impregnable position, guarded by precipitous crags on two sides. In 1155 William Peveril forfeited the castle, following his implication in the Earl of Chester's murder. Of the intervening years we have, unfortunately, very little record, but today the land once again belongs to the Crown. Parts of the original Norman building remaining include sections of the wall and gateway. Although the keep which Henry II built in 1176 is now only a shell, the surviving walls are eight feet thick and almost 60 feet high in some places. The internal area of the keep is approximately 400 square feet.

Standing among the ruins of this once mighty fortress the visitor who looks out across present day Castleton, Hope Peak and Devil's Gorge may try to visualise the scene as it was viewed by our ancestors through the ages. Perhaps it was such thoughts as these that prompted Sir Walter Scott to write *Peveril of the Peak*, the novel that has brought this castle of the Peak its relatively modern share of fame.

CHATSWORTH, HARDWICK HALL AND WINGFIELD MANOR: THE HOMES OF ELIZABETH HARDWICK

The Hardwick family had been lords of the manor of Hardwick for many years, when in 1520 Elizabeth, third daughter of John Hardwick, was born at the old manor house. At the age of twelve her marriage to Robert Barley was arranged; he was the son of a local squire and himself only fourteen at the time, but he was not strong and died a few months after the wedding leaving his child-widow a considerable fortune.

Still a very young and wealthy woman, Bess was sent to London where she met and married Sir William Cavendish in 1547. Now that she had moved up the social scale she turned her attention to finding a suitable home in her native Derbyshire. Having persuaded her second husband to sell his Suffolk properties, Bess and Sir William bought the Chatsworth estates and built Chatsworth House, the first of Bess's building ventures. In the ten years of their marriage Bess had three sons and three daughters, and in later years, she used her considerable skills to establish her children within the ruling class of the country. With Sir William Cavendish's death in 1557 Bess inherited all his properties despite the claims of his former wives; she then married Sir William Loe who died in 1564, and added yet again to her mounting fortunes.

Her final marriage in 1568 was to George Talbot, 6th Earl of Shrewsbury, who was high in favour at Court and was soon to be made custodian of Elizabeth I's problem prisoner, Mary Queen of

Scots. It is not clear to what extent Bess sympathised with the cause of the exiled Queen, but she was shrewd enough not to place in jeopardy her own position in Court circles. Socially and financially Bess's final marriage had great benefit, but it seems that her personal relationship with George Talbot deteriorated rapidly. After years of quarrelling she finally left him in 1584 and returned to her childhood home, Hardwick old manor.

Although now in her late sixties, Bess's delight in building was still very much alive, and she had plans developed for a complete reconstruction of Hardwick Hall. When her last husband died in 1590 Bess once again inherited a vast fortune and lavished much of it upon the rebuilding and furnishing of the new Hall which she had so carefully planned. Bess took up permanent residence at Hardwick in 1597 and spent her declining years enjoying the beauty of the surroundings that she had created. She died at Hardwick in her 87th year.

An account of Bess of Hardwick's achievements during her long life would be remarkable even today, but in Elizabethan times for a woman of yeoman stock to have reached such a position of power and wealth speaks of a determination and strength of character that must indeed command our respect.

CHATSWORTH

Route: A623 east of Bakewell; turn on private drive south of Edensor village. Opening:- April 1st to the first Sunday in November, Tuesdays to Sundays inclusive, and Bank Holidays 11.30 am to 4.30 pm. Mondays — Patrons only. Sundays only November to end of December 11.30 am to 2.30 pm. See also gardens page 18 and Farmyard page 22.

Built in 1553 by Elizabeth Hardwick and Sir William Cavendish, the first house faced eastwards. In 1686 the 4th Earl, later made the 1st Duke of Devonshire, pulled down this house and rebuilt a south front and later an east, west and north aspect. In the 18th century the 4th Duke worked out a scheme of reorganisation which involved straightening the river and removing extraneous buildings to allow a clearer view of the surrounding parkland.

Chatsworth is perhaps best known for the grandeur of the State Apartments and a tour will reveal paintings by Landseer and remarkable murals by Laguerre in the Chapel, Painted Hall and on ceilings of the State rooms in the South Range. (Other walls and ceilings are brilliantly painted by Thornhill). The State Bedroom ceiling is painted with remarkable landscapes which, although flat, appear to be sculptures in high relief. This room also contains the bed in which George II died. The State Music Room has an unusual door where 'hangs' a violin, attributed to Verrio but painted by the Dutch artist Vandervaart. Of special interest in the State Drawing room are the Mortlake tapestries dated 1635 and the coffers made from the oriental lacquer panelling removed from the wainscoting of the Dressing Room. The largest of the State rooms is the Dining Room or Great Chamber; the ceiling here, the Fury of Atropos, was painted by Verrio who is supposed to have represented the housekeeper at Chatsworth, who he disliked, as a witch.

The *Great Library* and its ante-library contain over 17,500 volumes in addition to rare manuscripts and prints, but perhaps the greatest treasure in this room is a bronze head of Apollo, circa 475 BC, discovered near Salamis in Cyprus. Beyond the Music Gallery is the *Sculpture Room* where in addition to the many sculptures by Canova there is also a fine set of hunting tapestries woven in 1450. Visitors leave the house via the *Orangery* and on to the gardens. See page 18.

HARDWICK HALL

Route: A617 S.E. of Chesterfield; turn onto secondary road at either Heath or Glapwell. M1 exit 29. National Trust Property. Opening: April to end of October, daily except Tuesdays from 1 pm; last entrance 5 pm. School parties Wednesday and Thursday only, 1 to 2 pm, advance booking essential. Refreshments.

Hardwick Manor was the childhood home of Elizabeth Hardwick and the ruins are still visible in the grounds. The Hall, as it now stands, was designed by Robert Smythson and Bess herself. A perfect example of an Elizabethan house, the Hall is remarkable for its external symmetry and for the vast expanse of glass, described as being of 'more glass than wall'. At the top of each of the towers are the large initials E.S. — 'Elizabeth Shrewsbury'.

The Entrance Court is almost perfectly preserved and there is an impressive line of colonnades filling the middle section of the fronts leading to the lofty Entrance Hall. This runs across the building, from front to back, a complete break with tradition. To each side of the plaster chimney piece hang large needlework panels worked in silk and wool. Items of Cromwellian armour and weaponry of a later date are on display.

The gradual flight of stone steps winds gently to the High Great Chamber with its wonderful plaster frieze depicting a hunting scene, the work of Abraham Smith. Eight pieces of Brussels tapestry, purchased by Bess in 1587, hang from walls designed especially for them. The great high ceilinged Gallery houses a further thirteen tapestries showing the Story of Gideon. Bess brought them from Haddon and had antlers added to the 'does' to turn them into 'stags' for her own coat of arms. Adjoining the Gallery is the State Bedroom, beyond this the Green Velvet Room and nearby the Scots Room (wrongly named as Mary Queen of Scots died four years before Hardwick was built). In the Blue Room there are again Brussels tapestries which blend well with the blue needle-point hanging on the bed. On the Chapel landing is the original fine glass lantern, later copies of which are hanging in various other parts of the house.

Among the many beautiful portraits at Hardwick is one very detailed painting of Queen Elizabeth the First; another is a portrait of Bess herself, probably painted about the time the house was built.

Hardwick Hall took seven years to build and Bess died there in 1607 in her 87th year. Standing much as she left it, the house contains a great many pieces of the original furniture and, of particular interest, the items of needlework carried out by Mary Queen of Scots during her enforced stay at Wingfield Manor.

WINGFIELD MANOR
Route: B6013, off A61 south of Chesterfield and north of Pentrich village. Admission on application to the owner at the farm house.

Wingfield Manor stands on a hill top; it is not just a home but a fortress, built around two courtyards. To the left of the outer entrance is a magnificent barn with fine old timbers. Crossing the outer courtyard, visitors will see the modern farmhouse built within the ancient external walls. Passing through the entrance gate to the northern quadrangle the grandeur of the orginal building can be appreciated. The massive tower, 72 feet high, dominates the west side and adjoining this are the curtain walls which retain almost their full height.

It was here in 1569 that Mary Queen of Scots had her apartments when held prisoner, at the instigation of Queen Elizabeth I, by the Earl of Shrewsbury, husband of Bess of Hardwick. Apparently Mary did not find Wingfield conducive to her health and she was moved to Chatsworth, Sheffield, Tutbury Castle and in 1584, back to Wingfield. There is a legend which maintains that Anthony Babbington, who lived at nearby Dethick Hall and had been one of Mary's pages at Sheffield, often visited her in disguise during her second period of imprisonment at the Manor. After the ill-fated Babbington Plot poor Mary was taken to Fotheringay where she was executed in 1587.

In the north-east corner are the remains of the mighty banqueting hall with a unique crypt or undercroft. The fine ribbed arches and traceried bosses are excellent examples of the period.

HADDON HALL
Route: A6 south of Bakewell. Opening: 1st April to end of September, Tuesday to Saturday inclusive, 11 am to 6 pm. Bank Holiday Sundays 2 pm to 6 pm. Bank Holiday Mondays 11 am to 6 pm. Refreshments available. See also the gardens page 19.

Only four families have lived at Haddon Hall, which was mentioned in the Domesday Survey. The first recorded owner was William Peveril. In 1153 the property passed to William Avenal and in 1170 was inherited by his son-in-law, Richard Vernon. Of this early period only the Peveril Tower and Chapel remain. Richard made additions and under licence built a 12 foot wall round the house, portions of which can still be seen.

For nearly 200 years the Hall remained unaltered, then between

1370 and 1426 the Banqueting Hall, kitchens, rooms round the upper courtyard, north-west gate tower and buildings along the west front were added. The last Vernon to live at Haddon was Sir George, a colourful character known as 'King of the Peak'. Tradition cast him in the role of an 'unfeeling father' who tried to prevent his daughter's marriage to John Manners. After her father's death in 1567 Sir John and Lady Dorothy Manners inherited the property.

By 1641 when a John Manners succeeded to the Earldom of Rutland the family were living most of the time at Belvoir Castle. After 1703 Haddon ceased to be occupied and remained empty until early in this century, when the 9th Duke made it his life's work to restore the Hall to its former appearance. As a result Haddon is now one of the most authentic specimens of a medieval great house.

Space does not allow a full description, but the most impressive rooms are the Great Banqueting Hall, with minstrel's gallery and lofty timbered roof. The stairs leading from the Hall have an unusual pair of dog-gates at the top to prevent animals from wandering at will through the house. The Chapel has a Norman pillar and font and some interesting medieval murals depicting St. Nicholas, to whom it is dedicated, and St. Christopher.

Built in 1500, the Dining Room contains fine Tudor panelling and

The dog-gates at Haddon Hall

13

the ceiling retains the original red and white paintings. The fine timbering of the Great Chamber also dates from this time. Haddon oak provided the flooring for the Long Gallery, a room 110 feet long by 17 feet wide, with many windows and alcoves giving it a light and airy atmosphere. It is considered the most beautiful room in the house; the delicate and intricately carved panelling incorporates the Manners and Vernon crests. Over the fireplace hangs a large painting by Whistler showing the 9th Duke with his son, the present Duke, as a boy, with Haddon Hall in the distance. The Gallery is strongly associated with Dorothy Vernon's elopement story, for it was from here that she fled, leaving her sister's wedding ball and ran, via the Ante-Room and the Dorothy Vernon Steps, to where John Manners waited with horses by the old foot bridge.

KEDLESTON HALL

Route: On secondary road off A52 N.W. of Derby. Opening: Easter Sunday, Monday and Tuesday, then every Sunday from the last Sunday in April to the last in September. Also Bank Holiday Mondays and Tuesdays. House and Museum 2 to 6 pm. Private parties by prior arrangement. Refreshments. For the gardens see page 19.

The first Curzon came to England with William the Conqueror and the family held land at Kedleston from that time onward. Church records dating back to 1198 show that land holdings were divided between two sons and that the present line of owners is directly descended from Thomas de Curzon who took Kedleston as his share. Almost nothing is known of the medieval hall which once stood on the site, but a survey dated 1657 records a doorway which was even then 500 years old, and mention was also made of a large hall and buttery with painted armorial glass.

At the end of the 17th century Kedleston old house was demolished and replaced by a square, three storeyed red brick building. This in turn was also pulled down, together with much of the old village, when Sir Nathaniel Curzon inherited the estate. Most of the village was re-established on its present site, half a mile away, but the church remains within the grounds.

The Hall reflects the work of two great architects, James Paine, who designed the north-east wing, and Robert Adam who continued the interior and decoration within Paine's structural plan and also designed the south front. The principal rooms are grouped round the great Ceremonial Entrance Hall which has a distinctly Roman atmosphere with twenty vast columns and pilasters of local veined alabaster. The hall is entirely top-lit leaving the walls unbroken by windows. To the east of the hall is the Music Room containing part of Sir Nathaniel's extensive collection of paintings. The fireplaces here and in the State Bedroom are inlaid with Blue John. Through-out Kedleston, Adam's influence can be seen, each room a master-piece of design and colour; no more so than the Saloon, a rotunda

Kedleston Hall

whose dome reaches a height of 62 feet, and the State Dining Room, with a semi-domed apsidal end, still containing the original furniture with curved tables especially designed to fit.

A small Indian museum contains exhibits of silver, ivory, ancient weapons and oriental art collected by Marquess Curzon while Viceroy of India. Also displayed are Adam's original drawings for the interior and exterior of Kedleston Hall.

MELBOURNE HALL
Route: A514/B587. 8 miles south of Derby. Opening: From mid-April to the end of September, Wednesdays, Thursdays and Sundays 2 to 6 pm. Bank Holiday weekends, Saturday to Tuesday, 11 am to 6 pm. July and August open daily except Friday and Mondays. Private parties by arrangement. Refreshments.

The first records of Melbourne Hall show that it belonged to the Bishops of Carlisle, as rectors of Melbourne, and the courtyard and coach house date from this period. In the early 17th century Sir John Coke leased the Hall from the Bishops and spent as much time there as his position as Principal Secretary to Charles I would allow. The Hall passed by inheritance to Thomas Coke, Vice Chamberlain to Queen Anne. He was responsible for the building of the east

15

facade and for laying out the gardens. Marriage brought the Hall to the Lamb family — Peniston Lamb, when given a peerage in 1770, took the title of Lord Melbourne. His son William became Queen Victoria's Prime Minister and gave his name to the new Australian city.

In the Entrance Hall, which was built at the beginning of the present century, stands the flag of the Australian Merchant Navy, presented to the 12th Marquess to celebrate the centenary of the naming of Melbourne city. An interesting document — a Grant of Land, bearing the Great Seal of Charles I — can be seen in the Serving Room. The Dining Room was restored in 17th century with small oak panelling and linenfold border. Much of the furniture is, however, of a later date.

Most of the books in the Library were collected by George Lamb, Lord Melbourne's younger brother; this room also contains several drawings by Gainsborough and Rembrandt. Three very large portraits of Queen Anne, King George I and Prince George of Denmark painted by Sir Godfrey Kneeler dominate the Drawing Room; much of the furniture is of the 17th and 18th century. Upstairs, Lord Melbourne's Room contains the round library table which he always used as a desk, and above it hangs his portrait. Many of the items in this room are reminders of the family's close association with Queen Victoria during his term of office as Prime Minister. Lady Palmerston's Room, Sir John Coke's room and the House Chapel complete the rooms open to the public on the upper floor. See also the gardens page 21.

SUDBURY HALL

National Trust. Route A50 west of Derby. Opening: April 1st to end of October. Wednesday to Sunday inclusive and Bank Holiday Mondays (closed Good Friday). 1 to 5.30 pm, or sunset if earlier. Last admission 5 pm. Special facilities are available for schools. Telephone Sudbury (028 378) 305. Refreshments.

Although estates at Sudbury had been held by the Vernon family for 100 years, the first small manor house was not built until 1613. However, the new owners never lived there and it was not until 1659 that Sudbury became a home. A survey made of the estate for George Vernon shows the site of the first house to the east of the present-day Hall. For forty-three years he concerned himself building, decorating and improving the layout, not only of the Hall, but the grounds and village as well. Sudbury remained in the family until 1967 when, on the death of the 9th Lord Vernon, it was presented to the National Trust.

The Hall is roughly E-shaped and the central feature of the north front is very impressive, with Doric columns and round and diamond shaped brooches. The interior is renowned for its beautiful plasterwork ceilings and intricate 17th century carvings on the Great

Staircase. To Grindling Gibbons is attributed the fine carving over the chimneypiece of the Drawing Room.

Queen Adelaide, consort of William IV, leased Sudbury in 1840 and the 'Queen's Room' — a state bedroom — remains almost as she knew it. To find a Long Gallery in a house of Charles II period is thought unusual, but the room is impressive with its intricately patterned ceiling contrasting with the simple design of the wall panelling. Among the large collection of paintings are many portraits of the Vernon family.

Between March and September various events including an outdoor theatre festival are arranged.

The unusual Children's Museum is described on page 45.

Sudbury Hall

2.

Gardens

GARDENS OPEN TO THE PUBLIC DAILY

Bamford - High Peak Garden Centre, Hope Valley (The Clifford Proctor Nurseries). Route: A625 two miles west of Hathersage, 4 miles east of Castleton. Admission free.

The gardens cover seven and a half acres presenting a complete horticultural service within the garden atmosphere. Over 8,000 roses are exhibited together with rock and heather plants, trees, shrubs, herbaceous borders and display hedges. A snack bar is provided at weekends. During the summer months visitors may also see a camping and swimming pool exhibition. Car parking is free.

Brailsford — Ednaston Manor. Route: West of Brailsford on the A52 Derby to Ashbourne road. Open daily except Mondays and Saturdays from 1 - 4.30 pm. Sundays from 2 - 6 pm. Admission free. Teas available on Sundays and on weekdays for coaches by arrangement. Tel. Brailsford 325.

Designed by Sir Edwin Lutyens the manor was built early this century, the gardens not reaching their full potential until the 1950s. Visitors will discover a wide range of trees and flowering shrubs, including a collection of acers, sorbus, rhododendrons, azaleas and old-fashioned roses, each one clearly labelled. Should visitors wish they may purchase container-grown plants from the nursery area. The gardens are suitable for wheelchairs.

Chatsworth (The Duke of Devonshire). Route: A623 east of Bakewell. Visitors to the gardens enter through Flora's Temple to the east of the House entrance. Opening: daily 11.30 am to 5 pm from early April to end of October. Sundays only November and December 11.30 am to 3 pm, including Boxing Day and New Year's Day. (The gardens are closed during the Country Fair in September and the Horse Trials in October).

Little remains of the garden Bess of Hardwick knew except for Queen Mary's Bower situated between the river and the house and the fortress-like Hunting Tower, on the hill overlooking the Rose Garden. Two major influences in the design of the gardens were Capability Brown and Sir Joseph Paxton. Everywhere broad vistas give way to hidden corners of beauty. Paths lead to the famous cascade and the Temple, where even the dome is a waterfall.

From inside there is a spectacular view, through the spray, of the house with the Derwent valley beyond. The maze was originally the site of Paxton's Great Conservatory, completed in 1839 and a forerunner of the Crystal Palace; his distinctive design can still be seen in the 'Conservative Wall' glass cases which house the beautiful Chatsworth camelias. He also designed the magnificent Emperor Fountain which can throw a jet of water to a height of 290 feet. The gardens offer a profusion of colour and beauty to the visitor all the year with drifts of daffodils, rose gardens and herbaceous borders. The many rare trees and shrubs are of great interest to the botanist and ornithologists will delight in the many species of birds to be found. A complete tour of the gardens will take at least an hour. A plan giving alternative routes is available; this also indicates easy and more difficult routes to traverse.

Derby - Kedleston Hall (Viscount Scarsdale). Route: as for the Hall. Opening: Easter Sunday, Monday and Tuesday and then every Sunday from the end of April to the end of September, also Bank Holiday Mondays and Tuesdays. Park, gardens and church 12.30 to 6 pm. Free coach and car park. Gift shop. Refreshments.

Robert Adam designed much of the Hall and many of the buildings in the 500 acre park including the attractive three-arched bridge over Cutler Brook, the boat house, fishing house, summer house and orangery. Everywhere a sense of peace and space prevails with sweeping lawns framed by banks of flowering shrubs, herbaceous borders and roses.

Haddon Hall (The Duke of Rutland). Route as for the Hall. Opening: from the 1st April to 30th September, Tuesday to Saturday, 11 am to 6 pm. Closed Sundays and Mondays except for Bank Holiday Sundays 2 to 6 pm. Mondays 11 am to 6 pm.

The gardens of Haddon have been described as 'of exquisite beauty'. Dorothy Vernon's Walk is linked to the lower terraces by a flight of 76 steps and flanked by balustrades over three hundred years old. In summer the mellow stone of the Hall affords a fitting background for the profusion of rambler, bush and climbing roses for which the gardens are renowned. Lawns, herbaceous borders and topiary trees complete the picture.

Hardwick Hall (National Trust). Route as for the Hall. Opening: daily from April to the end of October, 12 noon to 5.30 pm.

Still of original Elizabethan design, the walled gardens of Hardwick are a delight to the visitor. South of the Hall the main garden is of typical radial design with neatly clipped low hedges and gravel paths defining the quarters. Of particular interest is the National Trust's largest herb garden, mainly of a culinary nature. Many herbs can be purchased in the shop.

Lea - Lea Rhododendron Gardens. Route: 5 miles S.E. of Matlock. Open daily 1st April - 31st July, 10 am - 7 pm.

The garden is devoted almost entirely to different types of rhododendron; there are over 400 species and hybrids on display. The rock garden, planted on the site of an old quarry, gains character from the amount of outcrop stone which can still be seen and enhances the display of acers, alpines and dwarf conifers. Plants may be purchased and refreshments are available.

GARDEN OPEN ON SPECIFIC DATES AND AT OTHER TIMES BY APPOINTMENT

Apperknowle: The Limes, Crow Lane. (Mr & Mrs W. Belton). Opening fortnightly from early May to end of August. Route: From A61 at Unstone turn east for 1 mile to Apperknowle. First house past Unstone Grange. Telephone Dronfield (0246) 412338. A garden of 2½ acres with daffodils and spring plants; herbaceous borders, roses, flowering shrubs, geraniums and summer bedding plants. There are lily ponds with ornamental bridges and a further large natural pond where waterfowl and birds can be seen. Aviaries contain various species of pheasant and budgerigars; of added interest are the donkeys and Jacob sheep. Demonstrations of spinning, weaving and lace making are arranged and details will be found in the local press. Home made teas are provided. Visitors are asked to keep dogs on a lead.

GARDENS OPEN ON CERTAIN DAYS ONLY (DETAILS OF ACTUAL DATES MAY BE FOUND IN THE LOCAL PRESS)

Ashbourne—Parwich Hall. Route: East of A515, north of Ashbourne. This is a terraced garden, especially beautiful in the spring when the daffodils are in flower. There is also a rock garden.

Calver—Brookside Bird Garden (G.R. Pryor, Esq.) Route: In the centre of the village on the A622 north of Bakewell. The gardens are open on four Saturday afternoons during the summer and by appointment for bird, horticultural and photography clubs, for whom entrance is free. Covering about 2 acres the gardens contain many unusual shrubs and trees which, together with ponds, form a natural background for the collection of waterfowl, pheasants, macaws and other parrot species, cranes and flamingoes.

Darley Dale—Darley House (Mr and Mrs G.H. Briscoe). Route: Off A6 north-west of Matlock. Originally laid out by Sir Joseph Paxton the garden is of about 1¼ acres. The present patio indicates the site of the conservatory built to test the viability of his ideas for the design of the Crystal Palace, for the Great Exhibition of 1851. The present owners are restoring the garden which contains many rare trees and shrubs.

Derby—Radburne Hall. Route: 5 miles west of Derby, on the A52 Derby-Ashbourne road, turn off Radburne Lane. The Hall, though not open to the public, is an impressive seven-bay Palladian mansion. The large landscaped garden includes shrubs and rose terraces, and of special interest an ice-house. There are many fine trees and a magnificent view. The garden is suitable for wheelchairs.

Duffield—Hazelbrow. Route: West off the A6 in Duffield. These gardens, which enjoy beautiful views, are noted for many features. Most notable of these are the extensive rhododendron woods, a large rock garden which has been created from a quarry, a terraced garden, a walled kitchen garden and numerous flowering shrubs.

Hopton—Hopton Hall Gardens. Route: 2 miles west of Wirksworth on the Wirksworth-Ashbourne road, B5035. These are medium-sized gardens with a particularly beautiful rose garden. There are large lawns, a Glastonbury thorn tree over 200 years old and of special note a wall constructed of six half moons. A Roman urn found in the grounds, bearing the name 'Gellius', is thought to have connections with the present family. The gardens are suitable for wheelchairs.

Langley Mill—210 Nottingham Road, Nottingham. (Mr and Mrs R. Brown). Route on A612 east of Heanor. Although the address is Nottingham, this small garden is in Derbyshire. All types of plants from alpines to trees and shrubs mingle happily with the collection of shrub and climbing 'Old Roses' for which the garden is known.

Melbourne Hall (Marquess of Lothian). Route as for the Hall. A beautiful setting for the Hall, the terraced lawns lead down to the lake. The dark yew tunnel, probably planted in the 17th century, is the oldest part of the garden. Everywhere there are inviting vistas taking the eye to the interesting 'Four Seasons' monument given to the family by Queen Anne; the 'Bird Cage', a beautifully intricate pergola in wrought iron, created by Robert Bakewell, a local craftsman; and the 17th century Monument Room. Almost hidden in a small rockery dell is the Wishing Well where an inscription invites the stranger to rest and drink the waters. Along the bricked walls are plum, pear and peach trees whose fruit can be bought in season from the small produce shops.

Shirley—Shirley House (Mr and Mrs F.D.Ley). Route: Turn to the west 5 miles south-west of Ashbourne on A52. Open daily 1st April to mid-May and Sundays mid-June to end of August. Collecting box. Daffodils in abundance.

Spondon—Locko Park (Capt P.J.B. Drury Lowe). Route: A52 east from Derby onto B6001 at Spondon. A stone mansion, probably one of the most notable houses in Derbyshire, built in 1730. The park was landscaped by William Eames, a pupil of Capability Brown, towards the end of the 18th century. There is an Italian rose garden, pleasure gardens and an interesting arboretum.

Tissington—Tissington Hall. Route: North of Ashbourne and east of A515. Open 2 pm - 7 pm. Admission charge. These large gardens include a display of roses and there are colourful herbaceous borders.

3.

Places of Interest

BUXTON MICRARIUM
St Ann's Well, The Crescent. Opening Summer 1981 from 10 am - 6 pm daily. Special rates for school groups.

In this exhibition over 40 microscopes, including special projection models, will give visitors a unique opportunity to examine the microscopical world. Living creatures and objects will be made available for study.

CHATSWORTH FARMYARD
Route as for House. Opening: daily from 1st April to early October, Monday - Friday inclusive, 10.30 am to 4.30 pm. Saturdays and Sundays 1.30 to 5.30 pm. Bank Holiday Mondays and Tuesdays from 10.30 am. School parties are requested to book in advance. Car parking and dog park. Refreshments available in the stables.

Situated to the north-east of the Chatsworth estate, the Farmyard is a working exhibition designed to show how the farms and woods of the estate are managed. On view are various breeds of livestock including beef and dairy cattle with calves; several different breeds of sheep; sows and fattening pigs; poultry; and a number of working horses including Haflinger, Shire and Shetland ponies. Farming and forestry demonstrations are given during the summer and there are several static exhibitions. An interesting area of woodland has been opened up and provides the Strand Wood walks — entrance is through the farmyard.

CROMFORD — CROMFORD CANAL AND LEAWOOD PUMP HOUSE
Route: A6 south from Matlock, turn eastwards at junction with A5012 for Cromford Wharf. Continue on this unclassified road for Lea Bridge and the Pump House. The Cromford Canal Society is a registered charity and charges are only made to cover running costs. Opening:- April to end of September on Saturdays and Sundays. Regular sailings at 2 pm and 4 pm. Weekday party bookings by arrangement. School preparation notes and a projects service available.

Originally built in 1794 to serve Sir Richard Arkwright's cotton mill (see page 49), the canal has been restored to use by the Society. Here visitors can take a step back in time with a leisurely trip in a horse-drawn boat. In about a mile, passengers see the first swing bridge, and High Peak Wharf is reached. Here goods were transferred between the canal and the High Peak Railway (see page 59). Immediately past the Pump House at Lea Bridge the massive eighty yard span of the Wigwell Aqueduct comes into sight, crossed by two small swing bridges. During 1981 a further 1½ miles of canal is being opened. Also new is the Cromford Wharf Display forming the foundations of a new museum.

LEAWOOD PUMP HOUSE

Guided tours can be arranged singly or with boat charters. The pump engine is under steam from April to October, usually on the second or third Saturday of the month, also Bank Holidays from 12 noon to 5 pm. Special steamings can be arranged at other times by appointment. Telephone Wirksworth (062 982) 3727.

The massive pump, installed in 1849 is thought to be the only beam engine unmodified and operating in its original position. In each cycle three and a half tons of water are discharged into the canal. Steam is provided by two boilers in the adjacent engine house which is dwarfed by the 95 foot chimney. After visiting the pump house, passengers may either return by boat to Cromford Wharf or walk down the tow-path to Whatstandwell or Ambergate.

DALE VILLAGE

Half a mile off the B6096 NE of Derby.

It is well worth the short detour off the main road to visit the remains of this 12th century *Abbey*, founded by the Augustinian Canons and handed over to the White Canons of the Premonstratensian Order from Lincolnshire in 1197. Only the gaunt frame of what must have been a fine east window remains and fragments of the surrounding wall. Nearby a barn has been built to protect the foundations of the *Chapter House* and other relics excavated from the Abbey. The key may be obtained from Abbey House.

The Church of All Saints, probably one of the smallest in the country, holds much of interest for the visitor and presents an unusual facade, being under the same roof as the adjoining farm house. This half-timbered building is known as The Guest House, and was probably built on the foundations of part of the Abbey in the reign of Charles II. A short walk past the house is *the Hermitage*, the ancient cave dwelling of a 12th century baker from Derby who became a hermit and carved himself a home in the rocks.

The Cat and Fiddle Mill which is to the west of the B6096 is a rare example of a stone-built post mill dated 1788. Rollers were fitted to the bottom of the wooden structure, with a track built into the stone to enable the mill to be turned by the wind. The posts to which the ropes were attached can still be seen. Visits to the mill can

Dale Church and the Guest House

be made by appointment from 1st April to end of October. Telephone Ilkeston (0602) 321548.

DERBY — BRITISH RAIL ENGINEERING LOCOMOTIVE WORKS

Visitors are welcome on Saturdays, except Bank Holidays, between 9 am and 2.30 pm by prior arrangement. Applications should be made to the Works Manager at least 10 days in advance, enclosing a stamped addressed envelope. Parties must be of between 10 and 60 persons. No appointment is necessary for open day; see the local press for details.

Children under the age of 16 are not admitted unless accompanied by an adult. Entrance is by the Siddalls Road Gate House only — a small admission charge is made. Visits to numerous shops covering an area of approximately 51 acres are included in the tour. The works build diesel engines, repair and recondition main line and shunting engines and overhaul breakdown cranes and track maintenance vehicles. It is regretted that visits to the motive power sheds are no longer permitted.

HARTINGTON, DOVE DAIRY

Route: A515 Ashbourne - Buxton road, turn west onto B5054. Applications for tours of the factory must be made well in advance. Parties to be of between 15 - 30 persons. It is regretted that, owing to the layout of the factory, tours are not suitable for children or the elderly. Short visits may be arranged during August and details should be obtained from the dairy.

At this dairy the famous Stilton Cheese is manufactured. Visitors see in a modern setting many of the traditional processes that have been handed down for hundreds of years. There is a chance to purchase the cheese at the end of the tour.

MATLOCK BATH - GULLIVER'S KINGDOM

Open daily except Fridays (but including Good Friday and Fridays in July and August) from Easter to the end of September 11 am to 6 pm.

Set in a park this is a model village with a difference — over 200 scale models are linked by a miniature railway system. In addition there is a further extensive collection of model trains, with sound effects; a Swiss Alpine scene with cable-cars and ski-lifts; a model car racing track and radio-controlled boats. In contrast full scale replicas in the spectacular dinosaur trail depict, with the aid of sound tracks, the story of early life on earth. Other facilities include an interpretation centre, adventure playground, snack bar and picnic areas. New in 1980 was the Royal Cave.

MATLOCK BATH: THE VICTORIA PROSPECT TOWER AND THE HEIGHTS OF ABRAHAM

The grounds and Tower are open throughout the year from 9 am to dusk.

The Heights of Abraham are said to have been named by an officer who fought at Quebec in 1759 under the command of General Wolfe. Whether or not this is true, the ascent is certainly steep, though well worth the climb as the views from the summit are quite magnificent. At the highest point stands the Victoria Prospect Tower. In addition to being a prominent landmark, the Tower also affords the visitor panoramic views of the surrounding countryside. Of special interest are the caves, see page 53.

SHARDLOW — THE CLOCK WAREHOUSE AND MARINA

London Road. Route: South-west of Elvaston on A6 from Derby. 3 miles from M1, junction 24. Open daily 10 am - 6 pm. Telephone Derby (0332) 792844.

The Trent and Mersey Canal was designed and built by James Brindley in 1866-77 to join the two great rivers from which it derives its name. Shardlow became one of England's two inland waterway ports and is now described as the country's finest example of canal reclamation and conservation. Built three years after the completion of the canal, the warehouse has a unique wide central arch which allowed narrow boats to discharge and load their cargoes within the building. For details of the exciting 'Canal Story' exhibition see page 45.

During weekdays, parties — with a minimum of 12 persons — may take a narrow boat trip lasting for about 1¼ hours from Shardlow to the River Trent and return. Advance bookings are required for evening or weekend trips. Charges include entry to the exhibition. Refreshments are available from the Lace Plate Restaurant, overlooking the canal. Long boats for holiday bookings may be hired from the marina.

WINSTER — THE MARKET HOUSE

Stone market house with ancient origins standing in the middle of the main street. Following traditional pattern the ground floor was open with five pointed arches — now blocked up. Owing to the decline of markets in the village the building fell into a ruinous condition. Restoration, using old material, was completed in 1905, and the building handed to the National Trust. Now used as an Information centre it is open from Easter to end of September on Wednesdays, Saturdays and Bank Holidays, 2 - 6 pm — sunset if earlier. Admission is free.

4. Craft Centres

ASHBOURNE: THE POTTERY, ATLOW
Open daily except Monday, 10 am till dusk.

Atlow Mill stands on the river Henmore four miles upstream from Ashbourne. In the past this old mill drew its power from the river and served the local community by grinding corn from the surrounding farmlands. Now, though the mill wheel no longer turns, the buildings are again in use and it is the potter's wheel which has brought them back to life. Nearby is a large barn which houses the workshop and kiln, and visitors to the pottery showroom can see the full range of products available.

BRAILSFORD

Here is not a craft centre but a craft village. There are over 21 craftsmen, more than half of them working full time. The old coaching station stables, which had been incorporated into the adjacent farm buildings, are now individual studios. Here the visitor will find Rupert Griffiths, woodcarver and furniture maker, and his son Peter who restores antiques; Barry Potter at his forge; and silversmith Phil Withers. Across the road at Dial Farm is John Hermansen's pottery; the photographic studios of John Thomas and Mike Stafford; lapidary skills displayed by Brian Thompson; and, next door, Jo and Ida Platt produce beautiful model cannons and field artillery.

CALVER BRIDGE — THE DERBYSHIRE CRAFT CENTRE
Opening from 1st March to end of December, 10 am to 6 pm, daily. Saturdays and Sundays only during January and February (closed Christmas, Boxing and New Year's Days)

A pleasant afternoon may be spent wandering around the comprehensive display of Derbyshire pottery and watching the resident potter at work. At weekends during the summer, craft demonstrations will include spinning, weaving, carving, paper making and brass rubbing. Regular exhibitions by local and national artists are featured in the Gallery. The 'Eating House' provides natural and home baked food up to tea time. Young visitors are welcome in the play-room.

DENBY POTTERY — DENBY

Route: A61 south of Ripley. Tours are arranged most afternoons and bookings should be made with Mr John Holmes at the works. Telephone Ripley (0773) 43641.

The present pottery is built on the site of the original kiln, set up in 1809 to take advantage of the fine seam of clay which is still being worked. Visitors see all the processes of stoneware production, each piece hand-shaped and decorated by craftsmen.

ELLASTONE, ASHBOURNE: THE YEW TREE GALLERY

Open daily except Mondays 10 am - 6 pm (January to Easter open only at weekends, other times by arrangement). Car parking available 50 yds behind the gallery in the church car park. Tel. 033 524 341.

The gallery occupies part of an early 18th century house and was moved to its present position from Ingleby in 1979. In the semi-cellar the arched display areas, hewn out of the rock, are an excellent foil for ceramics, wood and glass. Other galleries throughout the house are enhanced by unexpected nooks and crannies lending added excitement to exhibitions by some of Britain's finest craftsmen.

HEANOR — PENNINE POTTERY

Opening Monday to Saturday inclusive from 9 am to 6 pm. Sundays by appointment. Closed in January.

A small pottery specialising in selective hand made earthenware and stoneware. A fruit motif is hand-painted on individual items. Traditional slip techniques are used for the semi-domestic range and terra-cotta ware includes parsley pots, piggy planters and Cornish jugs.

MATLOCK — WHEATSHEAF HOUSE POTTERY

Open from 10 am to 6 pm daily except Mondays and Tuesdays. There are no parking facilities for coaches.

Situated adjacent to St. Giles' Church in an attractive 17th century house, the pottery has a changing display of items made on the premises. Individual blends of clay and glazes bring originality to the range of domestic stoneware which is hand thrown on a kickwheel.

WIRKSWORTH FRANK PRATT, OLD GRAMMAR SCHOOL

Traditional hand-made and hand-carved furniture is produced in this small workshop. Each piece is individually made and can be seen in various stages of construction. The majority of the work is carried out in oak but other timbers are used if required.

5.   Churches

ASHBOURNE: CHURCH OF ST. OSWALD
On A52 Leek to Derby road.

Beneath the centre of the tower crossing a well has been located giving rise to the supposition that this was once the site of an ancient Celtic church. This was followed by a Saxon minster and later a Norman church, remains of which are to be found in the north transept. Relics preserved in the church include part of a Saxon cross shaft, each face having a different design; two 10th century coffin lids; a Norman capstone; and a piece of dog-tooth moulding. A small trough found beneath the altar, a rare example of medieval times, is believed to have contained relics buried during the consecration of the church in 1241. The 13th century capitals of the nave pillars show some beautiful carvings and medieval portraits including one of Edward I.

The upper parts of the tower and the 215 ft. spire were completed about 1330. Near the statue of St. Oswald, on the west wall of the nave, can be seen marks of Civil War cannon balls, three of which are preserved within the church. The great east window of the chancel, given in 1390, contains in the upper part nineteen coats of arms including those of the Duchy of Lancaster and John of Gaunt. The twelve graceful lancet windows and the priest's doorway are part of the original structure. Dividing the north transept, the medieval oak screen incorporates a painted wooden panel of the 15th century. The profusion of monuments in the Boothby Chapel commemorate generations of the family since 1372.

BAKEWELL: ALL SAINTS CHURCH

Decorated with scrolls, figures and animals, the 8th century "Great Cross" stands in the churchyard. Near the south porch is another and later cross of the 10th century. The porch itself is almost entirely built of carved coffin lids of the same period, no two being carved alike. Norman work can still be discerned at the west end and there are traces of an old corbel table at the north side of the chancel. One of the earliest and most beautiful alabaster monuments, to Sir Godfrey Foljambe and his second wife, 1377, is at the end of the south aisle. Other monuments, also in alabaster, are to be found in the Vernon Chapel, notably that of Sir Thomas Wednesley, 1403, and John Vernon, 1477. Here also is the famous

Ashbourne Church

monument to Sir John Manners and Dorothy Vernon, his wife, of 1584 (see also page 14). Other members of the family are commemorated up to 1637. The chapel screen is a fine piece of 14th century carving. The ceremony of blessing the wells takes place in July.

CHESTERFIELD: CHURCH OF ST. MARY AND ALL SAINTS

No visit to Derbyshire would be complete without seeing the church with the crooked spire. Leaning up to ten feet out of true the spire was built in about 1400 to a height of 228 feet. The earliest part of the church was dedicated in 1234, various additions being made to the structure until the mid-16th century; major restoration work was carried out under Sir Gilbert Scott in the 19th century. Items of particular note are the early Norman font and the beautifully carved and fan vaulted screen in the south transept and nearby, in the Holy Cross Chapel, the ancient processional cross (both c 1500).

DERBY: CATHEDRAL CHURCH OF ALL SAINTS

The church is of ancient foundation and was raised to the status of a cathedral in 1927. All that remains of the Gothic building is the fine west tower said to be one of the best examples of the period in England. Built in 1527 it stands 214 feet high, the three stages being divided with bands of carving which add richness to the traceried windows and panels. The rest of the church of this time was destroyed, it is said overnight, in 1723. Re-designed by James Gibbs, architect of St. Martin in the Fields, re-building was completed by 1725. The chancel was again enlarged in 1967/68.

The tomb of Bess of Hardwick, Countess of Shrewsbury, 1520-1607 (see pages 9 and 12) survived the demolition of the 18th century and now stands in the South Chapel. The largest monument in the cathedral, it was made to her own design in alabaster with pillars reaching to the roof and richly embellished with carvings. Many of her ancestors are buried in the vault below. Robert Bakewell, who died in 1752 and is buried in the cathedral, made the striking wrought iron screen which stretches across the chancel

Our Lady of the Bridge, Derby

and side chapels. Much of the other iron work is attributed to him and is of exceptional quality.

A service was held in the church in December 1745 for Bonnie Prince Charlie and his army and is commemorated by the memorial in the south aisle.

DERBY: THE CHAPEL OF ST. MARY-ON-THE-BRIDGE

This tiny medieval chapel is one of the few remaining bridge chapels to survive. Although it is known to have been in existence in 1488, all that remains of this early building is the four light east window and some of the foundations incorporated into the original 14th century bridge. There was, no doubt, a toll gate beside the building and travellers stopped, at the chapel to pray for a safe crossing of the river Derwent after paying their tolls. It was in the chapel, some legends say, that the Padley Martyrs spent their last night before execution, and records show that it was on the gate that parts of their remains were displayed. Services are still held in the chapel which holds about 100 people. (See also page 34 for the legend of the Padley Martyrs, the Chapel and Padley Manor House).

EYAM: CHURCH OF ST. LAWRENCE
Off B6251 north of Bakewell.

The Celtic cross in the churchyard is evidence that there was Christian worship in the 8th century. A Saxon church was followed by a Norman building in 1150, which was in turn replaced about 1350. From the centre of the nave look up at the three original tie beams which, although not in their early positions, still have their carved bosses. Round the clerestory walls are unique mural paintings of the 16th century, now restored and showing emblems of the Twelve Tribes of Israel. The pulpit is Jacobean and the chancel and belfry screens are 17th century, made from the Stafford family box pew.

In the north aisle is the top half of St. Helen's Cross, the other half of which can be seen outside the chancel door. Hanging above the ancient Saxon font in the vicar's vestry is the lamp which, according to a condition laid down in 1252, was to be kept burning during services in St. Helen's Chapel. On a wall bracket in the south aisle is a 12th century wooden carving of the Virgin, originally in a Swiss Alpine church and recently given to Eyam. Below the figure, in a glass case, are copies of the plague registers naming those who died.

The carved chair belonging to William Mompesson, bearing the date 1666, stands in the sanctuary, and by the choir vestry is the plague cupboard made from the box that is thought to have brought the cloth carrying the plague germs from London. Near the south wall of the church is the table tomb of Catherine Mompesson, wife of the rector, who died of the plague, standing opposite is a memorial stone to Thomas Stanley, who survived. The wells of Eyam are dressed at the end of August (see also page 74).

Eyam is probably best known as "the plague village", where the rector, William Mompesson, and his predecessor, Thomas Stanley, inspired the 300 or so inhabitants of the village voluntarily to isolate themselves during an outbreak of the plague. This lasted for 15 months in 1665-66, during which time 260 people died.

During the plague villagers even shunned the church, for fear of infection from contact with others, and so Mompesson held services in a small nearby valley called "The Delf", now known as "The Cucklett Church". Mompesson's Well on the outskirts of the village can also still be seen — a stone trough constantly purified by spring water where messages and payment for food were left.

About half a mile along the Grindleford road a small gate leads into a field where the seven tombstones of the Hancock family are gathered. The stones, covered in soft green lichen, are perhaps one of the most poignant reminders of the plague of Eyam. The tragedy is commemorated annually on Plague Sunday by a service in the Cucklett Church.

MELBOURNE: CHURCH OF ST. MARY'S
On A514 south of Derby.

Described as a small cathedral the main building was begun in the time of the Normans on the site of a 697 A.D. church. Passing through the fine west door, with four recessed orders in zig-zag mouldings, notice the ancient groin-vaulted roofs of the inner porch flanking the west tower. The massive Norman columns of the nave, the arches decorated with chevron mouldings, and the clerestory above, are exceptional examples of the period. A spiral staircase in the southern tower gives access to the clerestory ambulatory or passage and connects with a further Norman stairway in the south transept tower. The foundations of three rounded apses from the Norman church were rebuilt into their present form in the 17th century.

Near the west end of the church is the 12th century tythe barn, with Tudor additions to the upper storeys. Melbourne Hall was built on the site of the original rectory palace (see page 15).

PADLEY: MARTYRS CHAPEL AND MANOR HOUSE
Route: B6001 from Hathersage, turn left at "T" junction onto B6251, in about a mile bear left for station and goods yard. Cross the railway and continue down the track to the farm buildings. The key for the chapel is kept hanging on the gate of the bungalow behind the chapel, and is available night and day.

Padley Hall, built in the early part of the 15th century, remained the family home of the Fitzherberts until 1657. It is possible to see from the ruins that the walls once formed three sides of a court yard, the fourth side being the Gatehouse with the Chapel above. Traces of the kitchens with the drain, which until recently carried water to the house, can be discerned in the west wall. Blackened stones show evidence of the fireplace. For many generations the Chapel was used as a cow-shed for the adjoining farm.

The Chapel today is one large room, the upper floor having been removed except at the east end where the original level has been retained and the altar stone, found among the ruins, restored to its rightful position beside the ancient piscina. The carved hammer-beams and the roof are original; the two windows set in the centre of the north wall were once the main doorways into the Chapel, and are immediately above the present entrance. All the glass is modern depicting members of the Fitzherbert family; Father Garlick and Father Ludlam, the martyrs; and Monsignor Payne, restorer of the Chapel.

In 1588 John Fitzherbert was arrested in the Manor House, betrayed by his own son for hiding the two catholic priests Nicholas Garlick and Robert Ludham. They were all taken to Derby Gaol where they met a third priest, Richard Sympson. The life of John Fitzherbert was spared, but the three priests were dragged on hurdles through the streets before they were hung, drawn and quartered. The heads and bodies of the three martyrs were set up on poles as a terrible warning to other Catholics; it is said that they were secretly removed and reverently interred. A special service is held in their memory each year.

REPTON: CHURCH OF ST. WYSTAN AND REPTON SCHOOL
On B5008 off A38 south of Derby.

The ancient foundation of St. Wystan's can be traced to A.D. 653 when Christianity was introduced to Repton, the capital of the kingdom of Mercia. An abbey for both men and women had been established by 660. The crypt was probably used as a mausoleum for the kings of Mercia and the inner walls may originate from this time, the recesses being made when the body of the murdered St. Wystan was laid in a central shrine in 850. To allow a flow of pilgrims past the tomb the two entrances into the crypt were constructed (the light-switch is on the entrance stairway). In 874 the Danes invaded Repton (the body of St. Wystan had been removed before the attack) and destroyed all the abbey buildings, leaving only the walls of the crypt.

Between 970 and 980 the church was rebuilt and dedicated to the saint. The crypt was vaulted over and the four great columns with their spiral ornamentation were built. The new chancel rose above and the Saxon pilaster strips are still visible in the outer walls. The Normans enlarged the church by adding aisles to the Saxon chancel and leaving the crypt as it is today. In 1172 a priory of Augustinian canons was established by the Countess of Chester which remained until the dissolution in 1538. Remains of the priory

The Crypt, Repton Church

are now to be found incorporated into the buildings of Repton School, most notably the gatehouse, the guest hall—now the school library, and Prior Overton's tower of 1437. A fine example of medieval domestic brickwork is the headmaster's house. A tithe barn, the underloft and part of the cloisters have also been built into the school precincts.

The church tower with its graceful 212 feet spire was completed in 1340 and the vaulted roof of the belfry should be noted (restricted access). The roof of the nave is 15th century as is the clerestory; the porch, of the same period, contains a Saxon Cross Shaft, a tombstone from the priory and a 13th century coffin lid.

The small museum attached to the school is open by appointment only (telephone Repton 0283 703339). Items show the history of the school and village. The most interesting object is a Danish axe head which it is thought was left behind during the sackings of 874.

TIDESWELL: CHURCH OF ST. JOHN
On B6049 north-east of Buxton.

"The Cathedral of the Peak" existed at the time of the Domesday Survey of 1085; re-building in 1340 was completed by 1400 and no major additions have taken place since. The chancel screen and gate, the carved choir-stall ends and the misericords seen in the north and south transepts are all of the 14th century. An impression is gained of grandeur combined with light from the beautifully carved tracery windows. In the chancel is the exceptionally fine tomb of Sir Sampson Meverill who died in 1462; the five incised crosses at the four corners are evidence that it has at some time been used as an altar, and in the centre is a rare brass symbolising the Holy Trinity.

To the north of the sanctuary is the interesting brass to Bishop Pursglove, wearing pre-Reformation Eucharistic vestments and bearing the date 1679. The two female effigies in the Lady Chapel are believed to date from 1300. The Layton Chapel contains the "Gabriel Bell", one of the original bells which rang until 1928. At the west end of the nave notice the fine groined roofs of the ringing chamber and, if the door is open, of the south porch. Above the porch is the "watching chamber" and on the stone door jambs are carvings thought to be consecration crosses.

The village well is dressed in July and blessed at an open air service (see also page 75).

N.B.: Persons wishing to rub the brasses in the church should make written application to the vicar and must report to him or the verger when they have finished. No children under 12, or older children unless supervised, are allowed to rub the brass. A fee is charged.

TISSINGTON: CHURCH OF ST. MARY
On unclassified road east of A515 six miles north of Ashbourne.

Dominated by the massive Norman tower with walls four feet thick the church has many features of that period. The modern porch protects a particularly fine doorway with a carved tympanum. In the 14th century the boys of the village held archery practice on Sunday afternoons on the south side of the church and the pillars of the doorway are well worn from the sharpening of the arrows. Within the church the features of greatest interest are the ancient incised Norman font and the chancel arch, unfortunately partly obscured by the large memorial to Sir Francis Fitzherbert, who died in 1619.

Five wells in the parish are blessed during the ceremony dating back to at least 1615, and screens are erected at each well (see also page 74).

WIRKSWORTH: CHURCH OF ST. MARY THE VIRGIN
On B5023 and B5035 south of Matlock.

A Christian church of the kingdom of Mercia in the mid-7th century has described the foundation of St. Mary's. The Wirksworth stone which probably marked the grave of an outstanding personage between 700 and 800 A.D. is now in the north aisle; it is carved with 40 figures depicting various aspects of the life of Christ. Much of the church is Norman, re-built during the 13th and 14th centuries, and well repays a visit. There are many fine carved stones showing the King and Queen of Hearts, Adam and the Serpent and the figure of a lead miner with his pick and kibble. The royal arms of William IV are carved in wood over the door of the choir vestry. A Breeches Bible, 1602, is in a case in the north aisle. Of particular interest is the compound brass to Thomas Blackwall and his wife Maud with 18 children, dated 1525. The alabaster tombs of Ralph Gell, 1564, and subsequent members of the family are to be seen in the north choir aisle.

Well-dressing ceremonies take place over the Spring Bank Holiday weekend. (see also page 75).

YOULGREAVE: CHURCH OF ALL SAINTS.
On B5056 south of Bakewell.

An impressive church of Norman origin, probably built about 1130, with massive columns and a unique Norman font with a holy water stoup attached to the side, supported by a salamander carved into the bowl. The 15th century tower is said to be one of the finest in Derbyshire; the nave roof is of the same period with finely carved bosses. In the chancel is the beautifully carved figure of Thomas Cocayne, knight, dressed in armour and dated 1488. The oldest effigy is that of Sir John Rossington, in the sanctuary, and believed to be of 12th century. In the north aisle stands the alabaster monument of Robert Gilbert with his wife, seven sons and ten daughters — the date is 1492.

Well-dressing takes place in June (see page 75).

6.   Museums

ASHBOURNE: HAMILTON HOUSE TOY MUSEUM, 27 CHURCH STREET

Open 1st April to end of October daily except Monday, but including Bank Holiday Mondays, 11 am - 5.30 pm; also Saturdays and Sundays and during the winter school holidays. Day and evening party bookings by arrangement. Special facilities offered for schools. Tel: 0335 44343.

This new museum is a must for children of all ages. Forts, lead soldiers, puzzles, early table games, optical toys, children's books and early die cast toys mix happily with an impressive collection of dolls from the mid-19th to early 20th century and dolls houses. For the mechanically minded there are two large working Meccano models and an extensive exhibition of vintage 'O' gauge model railways which are fully operational. Collector's items may be purchased from the small gift shop and an additional service is a doll's hospital.

BAKEWELL: OLD HOUSE MUSEUM, CUNNINGHAM PLACE

Route: A6 into Bakewell, Cunningham Place is off Church Lane, above the church. Open daily from Easter to October 31st, 2.30 pm to 5 pm. Applications for parties to view at other times should be made to Dr. E.T. Goodwin, 32 Castle Mount Crescent, Bakewell. Telephone: Bakewell (062 981) 3647.

Built in the 16th century, this Tudor house has preserved much of the original structure with wattle and daub interior walls and open timbered chamber. Originally a Parsonage House, built by the Gells of Hopton on land bought from the Dean and Chapter of Lichfield, it was converted into six separate cottages by Sir Richard Arkwright in 1798. Now restored to its original Tudor design, ten rooms have been developed as a folk museum. Exhibits include small fire engines, agricultural tools, toys and items of industrial archaeology. There is an interesting and well displayed collection of ladies' and children's clothes, some dating from 1810. Special exhibition weeks are occasionally held and details are obtainable from Dr. Goodwin.

BUXTON MUSEUM, TERRACE ROAD

Open: Monday to Friday 9.30 am - 6 pm; Saturday 9.30 am - 5 pm. Closed Sundays and Bank Holidays. Admission free.

The museum houses an extensive exhibition of printed material on local history together with representative prints and paintings of old Buxton. Many archeological finds collected from caverns in the district are exhibited and include bones of numerous animals — the mastodon, similar to an elephant; sabre-tooth tiger and hyaena to name a few. The extensive and well displayed exhibits also include 27 species of vertebrate animals from Pleistocene Age caverns at Creswell Crags (see page 47) and Longcliffe. Inscribed stones from Roman forts at Brough and Melandra together with material found during excavations of nearby barrows and tumuli are of great interest. The collection of rocks, fossils, stones and minerals includes examples of Ashford Marble, Blue John ware, glass and other ceramics. The new Art Gallery displays fine art mainly of the 19th and 20th centuries. A series of changing exhibitions are held thoughout the year.

CASTLETON: THE CAVENDISH MUSEUM, CROSS STREET
Open daily 9.30 am - 6 pm; dusk if earlier. Tel. Hope Valley 20642.

As the major centre of mines and caves in Derbyshire, it is only fitting that here should be housed the Ollernshaw Collection of Blue John, probably the largest in the world.

CHESTERFIELD: REVOLUTION HOUSE, OLD WHITTING-TON
Route: A619, B6052 north of Chesterfield. Open from Good Friday to the end of September. Admission free.

Although now known as Revolution House, the building was originally an old inn, called the Cock and Pynot, and until 1850 the inn sign used to hang across the road. It was here that the 4th Earl of Derby, the Earl of Danby and John D'Arcy met one night in 1688 and together formulated the conspiracy which was to put William Prince of Orange and his wife Mary on the throne of England.
Part of the old building still remains and visitors can see the blocked-up doorway which once led from the Little Parlour to the "Plotting Chamber". The original Plotting Chair is still in existence and is now on show at Hardwick Hall; however the museum has a replica on display. Another interesting item is the old salt cupboard which stands in the Main Parlour. In 1938 Revolution House was completely restored and at that time it was refurnished in 17th century style. Among the exhibits at the museum are a collection of manuscripts, books and illustrations relating to the house and village. These were presented by Mr C.C. Handforth to Chesterfield Corporation, to whom Revolution House now belongs.

CRICH TRAMWAY MUSEUM
On B5035 6 miles south-west of Matlock. M1 exit 28. Open Saturdays, Sundays and Bank Holidays from April to the end of

*October, 10.30 am to 5.30 pm, and daily except Fridays 10 am to
4.30 pm from mid-April to early September. Large car park, cafe
and shop. For details of weekend summer events telephone
Ambergate 2565.*

The quarry in which the museum is based was originally developed
by George Stephenson, who built a narrow gauge mineral line from
here to Ambergate, the junction of the North Midland Railway and
the Cromford Canal. See also page 22. Part of the tramway is built
on the track bed of this railway, and some of the original buildings
are still in use at the museum. There are over 40 tramcars built
between 1873 and 1953 from systems at home and abroad, and these
include a horse-drawn car, "Sheffield 15" built in 1874 and "Vienna
4225" built for New York's Third Avenue Transit System.

Admission charges include a return tram ride for about a mile
with a stop to see the Peak District Mines Historical Society display
relating to Derbyshire lead mines; entry into a special tramway
exhibition in the re-erected facade of the 18th century Derby
Assembly Rooms; and access to the depots to see the static tram
collection. To add authenticity an Edwardian street is being
developed with a bandstand, gas lamps and street furniture including the gates from Marylebone Station, London.

DERBY MUSEUM AND ART GALLERY, THE STRAND

*Open: Mondays to Fridays, 10 am to 6 pm; Saturdays 10 am to
5 pm. Telephone: Derby 31111, ext. 784. The museum arranges
holiday activities for children and also a schools service.*

The exhibits housed within this building are many and varied and
in addition to the permanent collection many loan exhibitions are
held during the year, together with lectures and concerts in the
winter. The Art Gallery contains the largest collection of drawings
and paintings by Joseph Wright, A.R.A. (1734-1797) and fine
portraits by Ernest Townsend and Sir Jacob Epstein. The Gallery
also houses over a thousand pieces of Derby porcelain. The interesting collection of 18th century salt glaze stoneware and the rare
examples from the Derby Cock-pit Hill Potworks should not be
missed. (See Royal Crown Derby Works, page 41).

Natural history is represented by an almost complete series of
British mammals, including the pole-cat, wild cat and pine marten
together with a comprehensive collection of British birds. A 50,000
year old skeleton, almost complete, of a rhinoceros is on display
with many other fossil remains including the head of the giant
Irish elk. Young people will particularly enjoy the small aquarium
containing tropical and cold water fish, and in the summer a wild
flower table.

Visitors are reminded of the connection with Bonnie Prince
Charlie and the 1745 rebellion by the oak panelling taken from a
room, probably in Exeter House, Derby, where it is said the Prince
decided to turn back with 7,000 men. Also in the local history

section is a shrove-tide football used at Derby in 1846 (see also page 72). Coins from the Derby Mint of 924-1154 and to the present day are well displayed together with many 17th and 18th century Derbyshire tokens. Domestic utensils, lamps, watches, leisure activities including musical instruments and toys are depicted by excellent exhibits.

The Archaeology Room has displays from the caves at Creswell Crags (see page 47) and Stanton Moor (page 47). Romano-British pottery known as "Derbyshire Ware", with models of the kilns used, is shown with items from the camp of Little Chester and Thor's Cave. Also noteworthy are inscribed pigs of lead from the Matlock area. Perhaps the most interesting exhibit in the Industrial Section is the unique scale model and running lay-out illustrating the development of the Midland Railway during the last 80 years.

DERBY: MUSEUM OF INDUSTRY AND TECHNOLOGY, FULL STREET
Open: Tuesday to Friday, 10 am to 5.45 pm. Saturday, 10 am to 4.45 pm; Closed Good Friday, Christmas Day and Boxing Day. Access is available to invalid carriages. Car Parking in town centre.

The museum was opened in the autumn of 1974 and contains two galleries. The first houses the Rolls Royce collection of aero engines from 1915 to the present day. Models of aeroplanes in which the engines have been used are well-displayed. The second gallery is an introduction to Derbyshire industries and covers a wide range of interests. Each display shows development of the trade with tools and working models. The clays used for bricks and pottery lead to the section showing the making of Royal Crown Derby Pottery. In the general engineering display there are models of Rolls Royce cars and steam engines. The textiles industry is catered for with actual tape looms and hand-knitting frames. Lead and coal mining together with limestone quarrying each have descriptive sections showing the processes in detail. After touring the gallery, a unique service is offered to visitors who can be directed to places in Derbyshire where the various trades are or have been carried out. This facility will be of especial interest to students.

DERBY: ROYAL CROWN DERBY MUSEUM AND WORKS
Route: M1, exit 24 south onto A6, exit 25 north onto A52. Admission charged to the Museum.

The first pieces of china to be produced in Derby were probably made between 1750 and 1756 at the workshops of Andre Planche. These early productions were mainly porcelain figures of humans and small animals. In 1756 Planche went into partnership with William Duesbury and during this period the range of productions increased to include "useful wares", i.e.: coffee and tea pots, cups, saucers and plates. By 1769 Duesbury had bought the famous Chelsea and Bow factories and many of their skilled artists and craftsmen were brought to the Derby works. As techniques improved so the fame of Derby china spread and tradition has it that in 1773, when Duesbury was visited by George III, the right to include a crown in the factory mark was granted.

Duesbury died in 1786 and was succeeded by his son William, often called "Duesbury two". Unfortunately he died within the next decade, the business slowly declined and in 1848 the original works were closed down. However, a small group of skilled employees working at the King Street factory kept the Crown Derby traditions alive until 1877 when a new company was formed at the Ormaston Road factory, and so full scale production began again. In 1890 Queen Victoria granted her patronage and required the prefix "Royal" to be added to the company's name. The Royal Crown Derby Porcelain Company today continues to make fine china and procelain known throughout the world for its high standards of design and quality.

Her Grace the Duchess of Devonshire opened the museum in May 1969, and here the work of generations of artists and craftsmen is on display. Exhibits include the magnificent Group of Isabella, the Gallant and Jester from the Italian Cemmedia Del Arte, 1765, and a figure of Shakespeare. One very rare piece from the Andre Planche workshop is a figure sometimes called "Old Age." Beautiful modern additions commemorate major events and royal occasions. The tour of the works takes the visitor through all the stages in the production of this fine china, from the preparation of the raw materials to the final decorating and firing. Visits to the factory and museum are by appointment only, and application should be made to:- The Royal Crown Derby Porcelain Co. Ltd., Ormaston Road, Derby. (Telephone: Derby 47051).

DERBY: THE SILK MILL INDUSTRIAL MUSEUM
Route off Full Street. Open Tuesday to Friday inclusive 10 am to 5.45 pm, Saturdays 10 am to 4.45 pm. Closed Sundays, Mondays and Bank Holidays. Admission free.

A water-powered silk mill was built on the site in 1702. This was superseded by Sir Thomas Lombe's larger, five storey building in 1717, all five floors being powered by one giant water-wheel. Industrial archaeologists consider it the prototype for the modern factory. Although badly damaged by fire in 1910 the present structure has only been slightly modified, with only two storeys.

The ground floor contains a comprehensive collection of Rolls-Royce aero engines from the Wright Brothers in 1903 to the VTOL of today. New types such as the RB211 are continually being added. Display panels illustrate flight from birds to turbo-jets. An 'Introduction to Derbyshire Industries' is the theme of the first floor and includes lead and coal mining, iron founding, ceramics and brick making and the textile industries. An exhibition of railway engineering during the 19th and 20th centuries is planned. There are special facilities for schools with lectures and demonstrations relating to the collections.

ELVASTON CASTLE ESTATE MUSEUM
Route: The B5010 Borrowas to Thurlston Road approached from the A6005 or the A6. Opening from April to October Wednesdays to Saturdays, afternoons only. All day Sundays and Bank Holidays.

This new museum is centred on the original estate yard of the castle and covers two acres. Displays and demonstrations take place in the old cottage with its garden, laundry and dairy and in the reconstructed craft workshops. Here will be found the wheelwright, blacksmith and farrier with the saddler nearby; the cobbler, plumber and joiner complete the craftsmen who would have been needed on the estate early this century. Of particular interest is a gypsy camp; a timber yard with working machinery; and an agricultural exhibition which includes livestock — a shire horse, pigs and poultry.

EYAM PRIVATE MUSEUM, 'LE ROC', LYDGATE
Admission by appointment only with Mr C. Daniel. Telephone Hope Valley (0433) 31010.

This interesting small museum contains documents, pictures and relics of the Plague. The history is given with the church, described on page 32. Other literature and prints depict life in the village through the ages. A local geology display includes fossils, mineral specimens, prehistoric artifacts and examples of the rare Ashford Marble. Of particular interest is the famous 'Hopper Ring' which purports to contain a piece of the 'true Cross' given to Anne Hopper by Richard III. Sick people touching the ring hoped to be cured by a miracle, giving rise to the superstition "touch wood".

GLOSSOP: DINTING RAILWAY CENTRE
Route: just off the A57 adjacent to the British Rail station. Telephone Glossop (045 74) 5596. Large car park, refreshments, picnic area and souvenir shop. Open daily 10.30 am to 5 pm. Closed Christmas and Boxing Day.

Nine steam locomotives are housed at the Centre, mainly in the Large Exhibition Hall. Passenger express engines include 'Scots Guardsman', 'Bahamas' and 'Blue Peter' and range down to smaller industrial types. An extensive miniature steam railway operates at peak holiday times. At least one locomotive is in steam each Sunday from early March to late October and throughout Bank Holiday periods when visitors are able to take a brakevan ride behind the engine. A special 'schools day' is held in early July. From time to time locomotives from other preservation societies visit Dinting and engines from the centre take part in mainline running in connection with British Rail. Further information is obtainable from The

Secretary, 15 Priestnall Road, Heaton Mersey, Stockport, Cheshire (stamped addressed envelope please).

MATLOCK: MODEL RAILWAY MUSEUM AND EXHIBITION, TEMPLE ROAD

Open Saturdays, Sundays and Bank Holidays, 11 am to 5.30 pm, also June to September weekdays 11 am to 5 pm.

The Peak District in miniature — a complete reconstruction of Midland Railway trains travelling through the magnificent scenery of the Dales. The contours of the countryside have been faithfully reproduced and the intricately constructed bridges and viaducts are correct in every detail. The exhibition is continually expanding and is a must for all railway enthusiasts.

MATLOCK: PEAK DISTRICT MINING MUSEUM, THE PAVILION, SOUTH PARADE

Open daily from 11 am to 4 pm (longer in season) and by prior arrangement. Special facilities for schools with the services of a qualified teacher.

Two thousand years of lead mining are illustrated within the museum and all aspects of the trade, from prospecting to washing, dressing and smelting the ore are depicted. Unique to the area is the section on mining law. Of particular interest to children are two climbing shafts. The most impressive and important exhibit is the giant water pressure engine made in 1819 and found at a depth of 360 feet in a mine shaft at Winster. Tours of the museum may be made in conjunction with a visit to the Great Rutland Cavern described on page 54, where underground workings and methods can be seen, and the Magpie Mine, with its fine examples of surface buildings, field centre of the Peak District Mines Historical Society. Details are on page 54.

RIPLEY: MIDLAND RAILWAY CENTRE, BUTTERLEY STATION

Route: 1 mile north of Ripley alongside the A61. Open: March to October inclusive Saturdays, Sundays and Bank Holidays, 10 am to 6 pm. Free car park, refreshment, souvenir and book shop.

Established to commemorate the Midland Railway Company, the Centre — which is a Charitable Trust — aims by means of a museum complex with an operating length of line alongside to portray both history and development. At Butterley station there is a collection of over 20 locomotives covering ninety years of development. Included in 80 items of rolling stock are two American-built Pullman car bodies, an L.M.S. Travelling Post Office, a sleeping car and a buffet car in which refreshments are available. From the buffet car a mini-ature railway runs to the site of the signal box and picnic area. At Swanwick Junction, a five minute walk along the top of the cutting, two former collieries are being developed into further large display areas. Eventually the working section of the line will run from Asher

Lane through Butterley Station and Swanwick Junction to Pye Bridge. Each portion of line will depict the different styles of the Midland Railway Company. A regular steam passenger service will commence during 1981.

SHARDLOW: CANAL EXHIBITION, THE CLOCK WAREHOUSE, LONDON ROAD

Route: south-west of Elvaston on A6 from Derby. 3 miles from M1, junction 24. Open daily 10 am to 6 pm. Restaurant.

The 'Canal Story' exhibition housed on three floors within the Clock Warehouse commences with an audio-visual display and introduction. Canal history is traced through all its stages, from the 'Dreamers' — Joshia Wedgwood and other industrial contemporaries who financed and used the canal, to 'The Builders' and 'Navvies' who constructed it and the 'Canal Folk' whose life and livelihood it was. Visitors see a full scale reproduction of a 'butty' cabin and blacksmith's forge and wonder at the ingenuity displayed through the models and dioramas which show the working of an inland waterway port and canal system. Further details of the canal and leisure facilities will be found on page 25.

SUDBURY HALL: MUSEUM OF CHILDHOOD

Route as for Hall. Opening Wednesday to Sunday inclusive also Bank Holiday Mondays. 1 to 5.30 pm. or sunset if earlier. Admission free.

In a completely new concept this museum brings reality to the past. Here children are encouraged to participate. They can dress up in reproduction period costumes and become part of an Edwardian parlour or Victorian nursery, or perhaps let their imaginations roam in the fantasty room. There is a playroom where they can play with the games on the tables and even a chimney to climb up - without getting sooty! Throughout the year special facilities are available to schools and information may be obtained from the Education Officer. Telephone Sudbury (028 378) 305.

WHALEY BRIDGE: COLES MORTON MARINE MUSEUM, CANAL WHARF

Open from April to October 9.30 am to 5.30 pm daily. Closed on Sundays November to March. Tel. Whaley Bridge 3411.

The museum and art gallery are situated in the canal-rail interchange warehouse, a building which is of great architectural interest. Items mainly pertaining to the Peak Forest Canal and Tramway and the Cromford and High Peak Railway are imaginatively displayed and include models, maps and paintings. Additional changing material is supplied by the Barge and Canal Development Association. The art gallery specialises on works with a canal flavour, including paintings by Alan Firth. In the same building is a chandlery and craft shop where a wide range of traditional canalware can be found. Long boats may be hired from the wharf and details are available on application.

Revolution House, Old Whittington

7. Archaeological Sites

BELOW we give some of the archaeological sites in Derbyshire easily accessible to the public, although in many cases the local landowner's permission must be sought. In all cases further information can be obtained from the Derbyshire Archaeological Committee, Brayshaw Buildings, Marsden Street, Chesterfield, or the Peak Park Planning Board whose address is on page 76.

ICE AGE

Creswell Crags. 8 miles east of Chesterfield. Extensive caves with low-relief carvings on bone. Interpretation centre and picnic site.

NEOLITHIC AGE

Arbor Low. Go past the farm and across the field, signposted, off the A515 Ashbourne to Buxton road. Open: daily from 9.30 am, Sundays 2 pm. Closing at 7 pm May to September, 5.30 pm March, April and October and at 4 pm November to February. Department of the Environment. Small charge made by access landowner. The circle stands on a platform approximately 160 feet in diameter, surrounded by a bank and a ditch. There are 46 prostrate stones forming a rough circle all of light coloured limestone and in varying sizes and thickness. Excavations at the south-east side of the bank revealed a Bronze Age burial mound 70 feet in diameter, and beneath this a six-sided cist containing calcined human bones, flint, a deer bone and two clay food vases. One of these vases was decorated with cord maggot and fingernail impressions. See Derby Museum, page 40.

Gib Hill Mound. 350 yards south-west of Arbor Low. A prominent barrow standing 15 feet high and thought to be a multiple-level mound.

Five Wells and Minninglow. Large collection of chambered tombs. Access by permission only.

BRONZE AGE

Stanton Moor - Nine Ladies. Nine blocks forming a circle. A burial ground thought to have contained a cinery urn. There are 70 other burial mounds in the area, also the 'King's Stone'.

IRON AGE

Mam Tor. Near Castleton. Iron age hill fort. Hut sites have been revealed during recent excavations. National Trust.

ROMAN OCCUPATION

During their occupation of Britain the Romans built a number of forts with a network of linking roads. In Derbyshire one came over Stanage Edge to the spa of Buxton (Aquae Arnemetrae) and was crossed by another from Glossop (Melandra) at Brough (Navio). An inscribed stone from here is exhibited in Buxton Museum, page 38. Caverns and mines worked by the Romans included the Blue John Caverns, and the Rutland and Masson Caverns at the Heights of Abraham described on pages 51, 53 and 54.

Melandra Castle Gamesley Park, Glossop — ample parking and picnic facilities. Excavations carried out by the Department of Archaeology of Manchester University have revealed an impressive military enclosure of about 5 acres with stone walls and gateways. In the centre the plan of the headquarters building and parts of timber barracks have been revealed. Traces of further timber buildings, including an official guesthouse, are to be seen in the external civilian settlement.

OTHER SITES OF INTEREST

Round barrows are to be found at Bakewell, on Burton Moor, Bamford, Baslow, Bunbell, Chemorton Lows, Great Longstone, Haddon, Hartington and Peak Forest.

Chapel-en-le-Frith: 'The Bull Ring', a Neolithic henge monument clearly defined.

Pilsbury Castle: two miles north of Hartington is an excellent example of medieval castle earthworks.

Taddington: on the moor, Five Wells Tumulus, double row of upright stones with capstones, mound covering to form chambers and passages approximately 20 ft. high. The highest megalithic monument in Britain, 1400 feet.

Wetton, Long Low: 2 tumuli, 540 feet apart. Linked with bank of earth covering a drystone wall. On each side of the bank are large leaning stones.

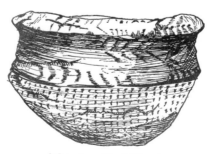

Arbor Low Food Vessel

INDUSTRIAL ARCHAEOLOGY

As one of England's main industrial centres Derbyshire can offer the visitor varied examples of working conditions during the 18th and 19th century, of which the following are excellent examples.

BELPER

Although now a thriving industrial town, it was in 1260 merely a hamlet of a few hundred people with a domestic industry making horse-shoe nails. Away from the main street a few cottage workshops survive. The town owes much of its prosperity to Jedediah Strutt, who in 1773 built a complex of cotton mills and workers' houses, now considered to be some of the country's finest examples of industrial housing of the 18th century. North Mill, which has been in continual use, was one of the world's first iron-framed fireproof buildings, erected in 1803.

CROMFORD MILL
Open April onwards 10 am to 5 pm, weekends 11 am to 5 pm. Tel: Ambergate 2287.

Sir Richard Arkwright, whose 'roller spinning' invention revolutionised the cotton industry, entered into partnership with the then wealthy industrialist, Jedediah Strutt of Derby, to build a horse-driven mill at Nottingham. This process was found uneconomical, and in 1771 a new larger water-powered mill was constructed at Cromford, modelled on the design of Sir Thomas Lombe's Silk Mill in Derby (a description is given on page 42). The mill is open as an industrial monument with exhibitions and displays pertaining to the cotton industry in Derbyshire. Details of the canal, built to serve the mill, are given on page 22 (combined tours available).

ROWSLEY: CAUDWELL'S MILL
Route: on A6 north of Matlock.

This is the only preserved example of a water-powered flour roller mill. Built in 1874, it has been carefully restored to working condition. Visitors can follow the full milling process and purchase the freshly ground flour.

Museums of particular interest to students of the industrial growth of the county are the *Elvaston Castle Estate Museum,* described on page 43, where the old castle workshops have been reconstructed to display many traditional crafts, and the *Shardlow Museum.* Said to be the finest example of an 18th century canal inland port, this museum traces local and other canal history in detail. Mining is represented by the Peak District Mining Museum at Matlock Bath, the mine workings in the Rutland Cavern and at the Good Luck Mine at Cromford, together with the surface buildings at Magpie mine. Details will be found on pages 44, 53, and 54.

8. Caves and Mines

THE mountainous region in the northern part of the county, incorporating the southern end of the Pennine Chain, is mainly comprised of carboniferous limestone. Through the ages water percolating through the rocks has resulted in the formation of a series of subterranean caves. During the Roman occupation these were found to contain rich deposits of lead, and to a lesser degree zinc, and it was lead miners who discovered the veins of Blue John, thought to be England's rarest and most beautiful stone. Other types of fluorspar are found within the caves, but it is the Blue John stone with its variegated bands of blue, purple, red and amber, which is of special interest. Although found only in the Treak Cliff and Blue John caverns, a small amount of the stone is mined annually and vases and other articles made from this stone may be purchased locally. Visitors should note that all the caves and mines tend to be rather damp, and a raincoat and head covering are advised. The long flights of steps to be negotiated and the rocky nature of the caves also call for sensible shoes.

BRADWELL: BAGSHAW CAVERN
Route: on B6049 south of A625. Open from 1st March to end of October, Saturday to Thursday, 2 to 6 pm. Closed on Fridays. November to end of February open for advance party bookings only. Telephone Hope Valley (0433) 20540.

There are two types of tour of these caverns. The first is to the Show Cave. The cavern is entered by a flight of 98 steps cut into the natural rock and leading into the old lead mine. From here visitors are conducted through a series of chambers hung with crystals and stalactites to a floodlit pool with interesting reflections.

The second, Adventure Trip, is an introduction to caving for beginners. Not for the faint-hearted, the tour includes chimney work, a long scramble down to an underground river, a mud and water pothole and an easy syphon. An experienced guide accompanies all parties. Individuals can be attached to groups and the minimum number is six. Cavers must bring their own torches, a change of clothing and stout footwear. Helmets can be provided. Applications must be made in advance.

BUXTON: POOLE'S CAVERN, BUXTON COUNTRY PARK

Open daily except Wednesdays, 10 am to 5 pm, from Good Friday to end of October. Educational groups by arrangement all year. Tel. Buxton 6978.

Although there is evidence that man took refuge in the cave for many hundreds of years before Christ, it owes its name to an outlaw named Poole — a Robin Hood of the 1440s. Roman tourists visiting the thermal springs in the town came to view the cavern, as later did Mary Queen of Scots, who gave her name to a large stalactite pillar. In the 1850s the Duke of Devonshire, who then owned the cave, appointed a custodian to prevent vandalism and run it as a show cavern. After a lapse of 11 years the cave was re-opened to the public in 1977 with modern spot and floor lights replacing the old gas lamps, one of which still remains — a reminder of the past. Visitors see the huge 30 foot dome created by a whirlpool during the Ice Age, stalactites over 100,000 years old and many others creating formations of breathtaking beauty and colour. The river Wye flows through the cavern for over 500 feet carrying water from the moors into the town.

CAVES AT CASTLETON

BLUE JOHN CAVERNS AND BLUE JOHN MINE

On the A625, opposite Mam Tor. Open daily throughout the year (except Christmas day). Summer 9.30 am to 6 pm. Winter closing at dusk. School rates available. Tel: Hope Valley 20638.

The entrance to the Blue John Caverns is reached after a short walk from the main road. Visitors descend to a depth of approximately 300 feet by way of a staircase cut out of the rock and consisting of some 200 steps. This is the beginning of one of the largest ranges of natural caverns in Great Britain, extending for over two miles. There is an interesting display of mining equipment to be seen including giant bellows which were worked by women and child labour to give ventilation to the miners below; an old rail trench; and a winch which was used to take the miners up and down the "pots" to the veins. Here may be seen the beautiful Blue John stone or "peakland Jewel" which was mined by the Romans and worked by them into vases. Two of these vases were later discovered in the ruins of Pompeii, and also one in Rome. The caves contain stalactites and stalagmites and a wide variety of shell fossils which may be seen embedded in the limestone. One of the principal attractions is known as Lord Mulgrave's Dining Room, 150 feet high and 30 feet wide, and with natural vaulting. This cave is named after Lord Mulgrave who was the leader of the first explorers of the caves and entertained his workmen to a feast here. The Waterfall Cavern, the Grand Crystallized Cavern sparkling with crystals, and the Variegated Cavern 200 feet high, are all illuminated to display at their best the rich colours they contain.

PEAK CAVERN

Situated a short walk from the village — take the lane which runs by the side of the Youth Hostel. Open: Daily 10 am to 5 pm from April to mid-September. Tel. Hope Valley 20285.

The entrance to the Peak Cavern is easily the most impressive of all the cave systems in Derbyshire. It appears as an enormous gaping mouth 102 feet wide and 60 feet high, while far above the overhanging limestone cliffs stands Peveril Castle. The visitor immediately enters a great cavern where the remains of an ancient rope walk may be found. Here the men of Castleton turned out hundreds of fathoms of rope, including the rigging for the ships which broke the Armada. At the back of the cavern is the entrance to an extensive cave system which includes the Bell House or Belfry (note the round holes in the roof); the Great Cave or Devil's Cavern; and Roger Rain's House, so called because of the water which constantly trickles down the sides of the rocks. The Orchestral Chamber contains a high ledge where a local choir used to sing for visitors. Beyond this is Pluto's Dining Room and the Devil's Staircase leading to five arches through which an underground river flows called the Styx or Peakhole Water.

SPEEDWELL CAVERN

At the foot of the Winnats, about half a mile west of Castleton on the A625. Open: Daily including Sundays, 9.30 am to 5.30 pm (4.30 pm in winter). Coach and car park. Refreshments are available. School parties specially catered for.

After leaving the coach and car park visitors pass beneath an arched vault and descend a flight of approximately 80 steps. They then proceed by boat along an artificial waterway, blasted out of the rock during the 18th century by lead miners. Although lead was never found here, many thousands of pounds were spent in the search which lasted for eleven years. It was during this operation that the enormous gulf the boat now enters was discovered. Here visitors may leave the boat and ascend a platform protected by strong iron railings which bridges the gulf. The height of this cavern is not known, as rockets exploded at 450 feet have failed to reveal the roof. From here also may be seen the unfathomable abyss below, aptly named the Bottomless Pit. The water which pours down unceasingly disappears for many hours, finally emerging only half a mile away at the Russett Well.

TREAK CLIFF CAVERN

On the Mam Tor road, A625, about half a mile west of Castleton. Open: 10 am to 4 pm in the winter and 9.30 am to 6 pm in summer. Coach and car parks. Light refreshments and picnic facilities are available. Special rates for schools, students, guides, scouts, etc. Guided tours.

These caves contain many beautiful formations of stalactites and stalagmites and rich veins of Blue John stone. The caverns were first opened to the public in 1935 and visitors are conducted down gravel paths through a series of caves 80,000 years old. Here may be seen the Fossil Cave with some fascinating relics from the Carboniferous period; the Witches Cave containing a splendid arch of Blue John stone; and a multi-coloured drapery of stalagmites in the Aladdin's Cave. The Dream Cave and the Frozen Waterfall, and finally the magnificent Dome of St. Paul's, are all illuminated to show the great variety and beauty of these formations.

CROMFORD: GOOD LUCK MINE
Open on the first Sunday of the month only. Other times by appointment. Visitors are provided with dust coats, helmets and caplamp. Strong shoes are advised. Adventure trips by experienced miners can be arranged on prior notice and take approximately 4 hours.

The Good Luck drift mine is unique. Described as a 'living museum', it is the only lead mine preserved in Derbyshire in which visitors may observe and experience the working conditions of a typical mine in the mid-19th century. The original mine entrance of 1830 has been re-built and it is through this that visitors start their tour. Guides explain the workings and demonstrate the uses of the tools and machinery which are cleverly displayed together with artifacts found during restoration. Examples of various climbing aids, wood and stone stemples - arch supports, sumps and raises can be seen. Above ground are restored coes - small storage rooms, a tub tipper, a dressing floor where the miner's wives and children used to work and other ancillary buildings.

CAVES AT MATLOCK BATH

CUMBERLAND CAVERN
Turn off the main A6 road by Holy Trinity church. The way is clearly marked.

This cavern was discovered during the 18th century by miners looking for lead. To reach it the visitor must walk along some of the old mine workings before entering the natural cavern. This penetrates for some 1,000 yards into the hill, and is noted for its striking rock scenery. Huge blocks lie scattered in disorder — one block of limestone is said to weigh over 40 tons. There are many galleries here, one containing a remarkable roof 25 feet long and 114 feet high.

GREAT MASSON CAVERN
The entrance to the cavern is in the grounds of the Heights of Abraham (see page 25). Open: Easter to late October, Sundays and Bank Holiday weekends, 11 am to 6 pm. Daily during August. Reduced rates for parties (on application). Guides tours.

As with the next cave, the Great Rutland Cavern, this was

originally a lead mine. The way is rather rough and is not as easy to tour as the Great Rutland Cavern. Hurricane lamps have to be carried to light the way, and the visitor enters the workings made by the lead miners. These passages lead to a natural cavern approximately 90 feet high, 220 feet long and varying from 12 to 50 feet wide. The walls contain many fossils and colourful minerals.

GREAT RUTLAND CAVERN

The entrance to the cavern lies below the Victoria Prospect Tower on the Heights of Abraham (see page 25). Open: From Easter to end of October daily, from 10 am to 6 pm. At other times by appointment. Reduced rates for parties (on application). Guided tours.

This is the largest of the caverns in the Matlock area and is part of an old lead mine. The mine was worked by the Romans, and many interesting Roman relics have been found here. It is of special interest to students of geology and Roman history. Originally known as the "Nestor Mine" it was mentioned in the Domesday Book. During later mining operations for lead the Great Rutland Cavern was discovered. The cavern is well lit by electric light, and being level is easy to tour. Visitors walk down a passage made by the miners into the hillside, and enter a natural chamber called the Roman Hall. This is more than seventy feet high and contains interesting rock formations. Also of interest is the Nestor Grotto. Late in 1980 a very impressive representation of lead mining techniques, contrived by a variety of audio-visual effects, was incorporated within the cavern.

SHELDON: MAGPIE MINE

Route: turn west off A6 three miles north-west of Bakewell onto unclassified road — steep hill — to the village of Sheldon. Cars must park in the road. Follow the footpath to the mine. Educational facilities available. Tel. Matlock 3834.

The mine is known to have been working in 1740 although it was not until 1810, after numerous setbacks, that it became profitable. It never remained so for long, each venture being thwarted by rising water — about five million gallons flow out of the mine each day. Today a tour of the surface buildings, said to be the finest examples of 18th-19th century lead mining in the country, begins at the smithy and agent's house, now part of the Peak District Mines Historical Society's Field Centre. Many of the original shaft entrances with their climbing ladders, the engine and power house, a modern reconstruction of a horse gin and other ancillary buildings can be seen. A tour of the mine combined with visits to the underground remains at Rutland Cavern (above) and the museum at Matlock Bath, page 44, gives a complete history of lead mining in the district.

9.   Country Parks and Walks

BUXTON COUNTRY PARK AND GRIN LOW WOODS

Over 100 years ago the 6th Duke of Devonshire planted the woods to cover scars caused by the lime quarry and today they form a natural habitat for birds. The rich variety of flora includes rare species of lichen, moss and flowers, all of which are well described in the explanatory guide to the nature trail. From the interesting temple folly panoramic views are obtained. Adjoining Poole's Cavern, which extends beneath the wood, is a modern interpretation centre. Here visitors may see a display of Neolithic and Iron Age items and Roman artifacts found in the cave. There is also an audio-visual unit, maps, surveys and photographs which members of the public are encouraged to use. Additional facilities include a picnic area, gift and refreshment shops and a free car park. Educational visits are welcome and details may be obtained from the Warden at the Park. Telephone Buxton (0298) 6978. See also page 51.

CASTLETON—THE WINNATS PASS

This spectacular pass through the limestone valley has gradients of 1 in 5 with hairpin bends and attracts thousands of people each year. To preserve the pass a traffic scheme has been evolved prohibiting vehicular traffic on Saturdays, Sundays and Bank Holidays. A large car park has been provided off the A625. Visitors may enjoy the rugged beauty of the pass on foot, although in some places this presents a stiff climb.

CHEE DALE

This is one of the dales cut by the river Wye near Buxton, and is a great favourite with walkers. At the foot of Tapley Pike the path leaves the road (A6) and passes a large limestone quarry in Great Rocks Dale. The quarry is fairly well hidden, and soon the grass slopes steepen and Chee Dale begins. The dale, forbidden to motorists, is approximately 2 miles long and the walk may prove difficult in parts, especially after rain when the path tends to be slippery. Beneath Chee Tor the scenery is imposing, the steep cliffs barely leaving room for the river. Despite this, trees, ivy and bushes cling everywhere. The dale finishes as Millers Dale station is approached and here the road must be followed. Beyond the station, *Millers Dale* leads to *Water-cum-Jolly Dale* and *Upper Dale* which finishes at Little Longstone. *Monsal Dale*, further on again, has quiet stretches with ideal picnic places along the path.

Lion Rocks, Dovedale

DOVEDALE

The most popular of the dales, Dovedale is only two miles in length, north from Thorpe Cloud to Hartington. The entrance is half way between Thorpe and Ilam—turn by the Izaak Walton Hotel. In 500 yards further on there is a large car park. The river must be crossed either by a little bridge by the car park, or later by the stepping stones—these are flat topped and safe. The path to these stones is surfaced, but from now on the way is rough, sometimes steep and frequently muddy. The path soon enters the trees and begins to rise, coming out on Sharplow Point opposite a crag called the Twelve Apostles. The path descends into the trees and beyond them, high in the hillside, are two small caves—Reynard's Kitchen and Reynard's Cave. The narrowest part of the dale is now reached, called the Straits. The Lion Rock at the northern end is an outcrop of limestone overhanging the path, so called because it resembles a lion's face. Beyond this, Ilam Rock, a tall pinnacle, is a most impressive sight. Dove Holes are two large arched openings in the cliff which mark the last part of the woods of Dovedale. The path passes into *Mill Dale,* and further on into *Wolfscote Dale,* which has steep slopes and wooded crags. At the far end of Wolfscote Dale lies *Beresford Dale* which though small is very beautiful, lying within both Derbyshire and Staffordshire.

ELVASTON CASTLE COUNTRY PARK

Route: Cars and coaches to the car park take the B5010 Borrowash to Thulston road, approached from the A6005 or the A6. For invalid carriages there is free access to the castle precinct via Castle Drive off Borrowash Road. Pedestrians should approach from Elvaston via Elvaston Lane, London Road via Golden Gates, or Borrowash Road via Castle Drive. Cyclists may park in the car park or in the stable yard approached via the bridleway. Horseriders may use the riding circuit accessible via the bridleways at Elvaston village and Oak Flat or from the Borrowash Road by Hartington Villas. Follow horseshoe signs in the Park. The Park is open daily— admission is free. A small charge is made for car parking at weekends and Bank Holidays.

The present 'castle' dates from 1827 although there has been a manor house on the site since the 11th century. William Barron, head gardener, designed the gardens in 1830. The Estate Trail leads through ornamental woodlands and topiary gardens; much reclamation work is taking place to restore the grounds to their original landscaping. The Old English Garden, open from 9 am to 5 pm, contains an interesting collection of climbing plants, wide herbaceous borders and, of special interest to the blind, a well stocked herb garden.

A new nature trail is in the course of construction and there is a wildfowl reserve by the lake. A field studies centre is run from the castle for the sole use of schools in Southern Derbyshire, although other schools are able to use the park. Other facilities available include a children's play area with the reconstructed gardener's cottage; picnic areas; a riding centre where lessons can be given to beginners, advanced and disabled riders—contact Mr and Mrs J. Staton on Derby (0332) 751927; and camping and caravan sites. A rural craft museum has been developed in the estate yard and details can be found on page 43.

THE GOYT VALLEY TRAFFIC SCHEME

The scheme operates on Sundays and Bank Holiday Mondays from the Sunday preceding the first Monday in May to the last Sunday in September, and is in force between 1.30 and 6.30 pm. Visitors are requested to use the free parking at The Street or Derbyshire Bridge where Rangers are available to give help and advice. Cars displaying disabled persons' orange badges are allowed access from The Street to use the Errwood Hall car park and from Derbyshire Bridge for Goytsclough Quarry park; other cars carrying old or infirm persons are allowed at the Ranger's discretion. A mini-bus service operates from Derbyshire Bridge to the Quarry park; a small charge is made. At all other times a one-way system operates from Errwood car park to Derbyshire Bridge.

During the last century the Goyt valley was a thriving farming community, Errwood Hall being the focal point. The Hall, built in 1830 by the Grimshawe family and now in ruins, had its own water mill, coal mine, school and cemetery. The extensive grounds are well worth visiting, especially in spring as they contain over 40,000 rhododendron and azalea bushes. The ruins of the workers' cottages may also be seen a short distance away. In the hills a small shrine built in 1899 contains a picture in Spanish tiles of St Joseph and the Holy Child.

The Goyt Valley, which includes the Fernilee and Errwood Reservoirs, is now an important water gathering ground, and also caters for many recreational interests. Visitors may be interested to see the old pack horse bridge which was originally used for smuggling salt between Cheshire and Derbyshire. This was moved upstream to its present position óver the river Goyt when part of the valley was flooded with the completion of the Errwood Reservoir.

WALKING ROUTES

Below are a few of the many interesting walks from the car parks and picnic areas. They are waymarked with yellow arrows. A number of these walks cross boggy, rough moorland and visitors are strongly advised to wear protective clothing and stout boots.

(1) From The Street to Pym Chair, along the ridge via Cats Tor and Shining Tor to the Errwood Hall Picnic Area, with an alternative route down the wooded valley of Shooters Clough. Return by road. Circular route, approx. 5¾ miles.

(2) A shorter walk from The Street towards Pym Chair, and down a wooded valley to Errwood Hall. Return by road. Circular route, approx. 2½ miles.

(3) From the Errwood Dam Picnic Area along the track below Hoo Moor to Oldfield Farm, returning down the western side of the Fernilee Reservoir. Circular route, approx. 3 miles.

(4) From the Goytsclough Picnic Area take the moorland path above the river Goyt, down the valley of the Wildmoorstone Brook to the Errwood Reservoir before climbing to the road at Bunsal Cob. Return via the Errwood Dam to Goytsclough Quarry. Circular route, approx. 4½ miles.

(5) A fairly difficult climb across moorland towards Shining Tor from the Goytsclough Quarry Picnic Area, before following Walk 1 down to the Errwood Hall Picnic Area, returning by road. Circular route, approx. 3½ miles.

(6) Walks from the Derbyshire Bridge Car Park include one along the old Macclesfield Road, across moorland and down Berry Clough following a path above the River Goyt to Goytsclough Quarry Picnic Area. The road into the valley is an interesting route to the Goytsclough Quarry Picnic Area, and beyond to the Errwood Hall Picnic Area.

HARDWICK PARK NATURE WALK
National Trust. Route as for the Hall. Access from the Ault Hucknell road. Admission free — a small charge is made for car parking. Picnic area.

This is a good long walk with plenty of interest. Visitors are asked to keep their dogs on a leash between the red markers. From the Visitors' Centre take the path over the River Doe Lea bridge; to the right notice the spillway of the Great Pond Dam. Turning left, pass the 400 year old Hardwick oak and continue on to Millers Pond, now being reclaimed. Many varieties of birds and water fowl will be seen here. Turning up the hill, away from the river, an area of natural evolution is entered, young oaks and hawthorn bushes giving way to forest where wild game is encouraged to breed. Follow the path over three stiles to Broad Oak Hill. Take a short rest on one of the benches and watch the herd of Friesian cattle and rare Longhorns grazing peacefully among the white faced Woodland sheep. Continue to walk down the hill to the drive; after the second gate take the path to the right into Row Pond Dumble and past a series of ancient fish ponds. After crossing the dam at the end of the second pond you will see the 'Ice House'. When packed with ice from the ponds this 'refrigerator' would last until summer. After the third pond the paths divide and a direct way can be taken back to the start. For the longer route climb the stile by the gate. It is *essential* to put dogs on a leash here as you are entering a wild life refuge; once over the fence with the white triangle, dogs can be let off. To your right stretches the Great Pond with its abundance of water fowl. After turning right cross the dam, noticing the sluices and spillway from the lake, turn left and return to the start of your walk. Tickets for fishing and boating on Millers Pond are available.

THE HIGH PEAK TRAIL

The High Peak Trail, 17½ miles long, links Cromford with Buxton. It has been developed from the former Cromford and High Peak railway line at the junction with the Cromford Canal, see also page 22, for cyclists, walkers and horseriders to enjoy traffic-free amenities. Car parks, toilets, an information centre, picnic areas and circuit footpaths are among the facilities provided by the County Council and the Peak Park Planning Board.

At Parsley Hay the Tissington Trail (see page 64) joins the High Peak Trail and continues to Dowlow near Buxton. There are many places of interest as the Trail follows a route which passes through contrasting countryside, from the gentle wooded slopes of the Derwent Valley to the limestone uplands and outcrops of gritstone.

At *High Peak Junction* there are a number of interesting railway buildings, including the former railway workshop and wharf shed. The *Sheep Pasture Incline* varies in gradient between 1 in 8 and 1 in 9 and is 1,320 yards in length. The *Sheep Pasture Engine House* still remains as a shelter and monument, but all the machinery has been removed. Further on at Black Rocks, a well-known beauty spot, there is a picnic area and car park. This district is popular with climbers, and there are also circular walks through adjoining woodlands.

At the summit of the *Middleton Incline* (gradient 1 in 8¾) stands

Train on the Cromford and High Peak Railway

Middleton Top Engine House which contains the only surviving steam winding engine from the original eight. It was built in 1829 by the Butterley Company of Ripley to haul wagons up the steep incline. The engine house is open to the public every Sunday from 10.30 am to 5 pm and at other times on application to the Warden. Tel. Wirksworth 3204. The engine can be seen in operation on the first Saturday of each month. Access by road is from the B5023 Wirksworth - Middleton Road. Car park, picnic area, toilets and Ranger service.

The *Hopton Tunnel*, 113 yards in length, precedes the *Hopton Incline* which, with a gradient of 1 in 14, was the steepest worked by adhesion locomotives in the British Isles. The Trail continues past Harboro' Rocks, where cave formations are said to have been the home of Stone Age Man, to *Longcliffe Station,* where again a few railway buildings remain, and on past Minninglow, Gotham and Friden until Parsley Hay is reached. Here the High Peak Trail is joined by the Tissington Trail. Car park and picnic facilities are available at both Friden and Parsley Hay.

Along the Trail coloured markers show routes of varying length to nearby local places of interest. Yellow markers indicate a walking route, and red markers a walking, pony trekking and cycling route. The Trails are supervised by Rangers, who will advise visitors of the many places of interest in the area. Bicycles may be hired from Middleton Top and Parsley Hay.

ILAM HALL, PARADISE WALK

National Trust. Route: At the junction of the A52 and A523 west of Ashbourne turn east, sign-posted Ilam. A small charge is made for car parking.

Ilam Hall, now a Youth Hostel and not open to the public, is situated at the entrance to Dove Dale and is an excellent starting point for walks in the valley, see page 56, and the shorter Paradise Walk. Leaving the Hall, go down the drive to the church where reminders that this was once a Saxon settlement can be found. Here also is the tomb of St. Bertram, who in the 8th century, overcome by grief at the loss of his wife and child, lived the life of a hermit. Across the field behind the church, inside a walled enclosure, is a clear water spring known as St Bertram's Pool, and nearby the bridge which spans the river also bears his name. To continue the walk stay this side of the river. Soon the famous Boil Holes will be seen; here the river re-emerges from its subterranean channel—the path becomes narrow and can be slippery. Further along, leaving the river to the left, the original gardens become apparent and shortly the way widens into Paradise Walk. To the right, protected by a rustic fence, is the Battle Stone commemorating a battle between the Danes and Saxons in about 1100 AD. Continue beside the wood until the footbridge is reached; here pause a while. Many rare and unusual plants and mosses are to be seen in the vicinity. Retrace the path for a short distance before climbing the track up the hill. From the top there are excellent views across the park to the Hall. The way now leads between the caravan site and the cricket field back to the Hall and Information Centre.

PEAK DISTRICT NATIONAL PARK

One of ten areas in England and Wales designated as a National Park, the Peak District covers 542 square miles and parts of six counties: Derbyshire, Staffordshire, Cheshire, Greater Manchester, West and South Yorkshire. The Peak Park Joint Planning Board is responsible for administration, conservation and liaison between the public and local landowners. To this end Park Rangers cover the area to give help to local people and visitors. We are indebted to the Board for the help and assistance they have given in the revision of this guide.

PEAK NATIONAL PARK WALKWAYS

These walkways have been prepared by the Planning Board in conjunction with British Rail. Paytrains from Manchester and Sheffield run direct to the spectacular Hope valley and the walks can be started from any of the stations named. Time-tables are available.

From Hope

1.   A moderately difficult walk of about 6 miles over Bradwell Edge to Abney

Moor, ending at Bamford station.

2. To the top of Win Hill with lovely views, five miles to Bamford station.

From Hathersage

3. A level riverside walk of about 2½ miles passing Padley Chapel (see page 33) and the mill, ending at Grindleford.

4. The south side of the valley is traversed in this 4 mile walk to Bamford station.

5. Longer and more difficult, this 6½ mile walk along Stanage Edge passes North Lees Hall, known to readers of Jane Eyre as 'Thornfield Hall'. Return to Bamford.

From Grindleford

6. An easy 6 mile moorland walk through Padley Gorge, part of the Longshaw Estate (National Trust) and Burbage Bridge to Hathersage station.

7. A short circular walk with spectacular views of the Hope and Derwent valleys. Although only 2½ miles a long winding series of steps have to be climbed.

THE PENNINE WAY (for experienced walkers)

The Pennine Way stretches for 250 miles from Edale to Kirk Yetholm in Scotland, the first few miles lying within Derbyshire. The primary route from Edale (where there is a Peak District National Park information centre) lies up the Grindsbrook Valley and across the soggy shelterless moorland to Kinder Scout. An alternative route is by Upper Booth and Lee House, where a pack horse bridge crosses the river Noe, to Jacob's Ladder. Steps cut into the hillside here make the ascent easier, and the path continues to Edale Cross, a stubby stone medieval cross. The two routes converge and pass on to Kinder Scout. Kinder Downfall is a small stream which rises at the summit and flows north and west before tumbling over the edge as a waterfall. Although in fair weather there is little to see, in rainy conditions it is most impressive as the fall is at the head of narrow cliffs. When the wind is from the west the rocks funnel the wind which scoops up the water and flings it high in the air as a plume, visible for many miles. From Kinder Scout the route goes by Ashop Clough and across the Snake road (1,680 feet). From here tall wooden stakes mark the Way across the wastes of Bleaklow. This drops down to Longdendale before returning to the moors above Crowden Little Brook and to Black Hill, where it leaves the county.

All access is free, but from the 12th August to 10th December some parts of the moors may be closed for shooting. Indicator boards are set up at access points and walkers should consult these. At weekends and public holidays wardens of the Peak Planning Board patrol the moorlands to give advice and help and can be recognised by their green or red armbands.

RIBER CASTLE FAUNA RESERVE AND WILDLIFE PARK
Route: B6014 from Matlock to Tansley via Alders Lane for 1 mile to Riber. The road via Starkholmes should be avoided as it includes dangerous bends and a 1 in 4 hill. Open: 10 am to 7 pm daily (4 pm

in winter). Reduction for parties of 20. Season tickets may be purchased. Parking and picnic facilities. Dogs are not allowed in the grounds but they can be taken into the car park and picnic areas. Light refreshments and souvenirs are available.

Riber Castle Fauna Reserve and Wildlife Park was opened in the spring of 1963. The aims of the Reserve are to maintain a collection of British and European fauna in their natural conditions and to breed as many species as possible to preserve and ensure their survival. The Rare Breeds Survival Trust has now established the park as an official centre.

Species to be seen from Europe include imperial eage, lynx, arctic fox, racoons, wolves, wolverines, porcupine, wild boar, whooper swans and waterfowl. The British collection includes a heron aviary, polecat enclosure, otter and badger pens, and barn and tawny owl aviaries. In large open enclosures are fallow and red deer, goats, sheep, pigeons, rabbits, red fox and ponies. The lynx centre is said to house the most comprehensive collection in the world; there are four species and from mid-July kittens can often be seen. In the poultry gardens rare and pure bred birds are being developed and are of great interest to the visitor. Riber affords an excellent opportunity of seeing our native birds and animals at close quarters.

New items are continually being introduced and include a display of butterflies, a model railway exhibition and a collection of farm vehicles. Housed within the castle walls is the museum of M.G. cars and Norton racing motorbikes. Details of these and other new additions may be found in the 'News Room' which has been opened in the courtyard. Riber Castle, though only a shell, is still most impressive with four tall corner towers. The building stands on top of steep cliffs and can be seen for many miles.

SETT VALLEY TRAIL
Route: on A625 to Hayfield or A6015 from New Mills. Parking at the station. Picnic area. Toilets. Ranger post and Information Room. At Torr Top, New Mills: car park and toilets, information board.

The old Hayfield railway line provides a traffic-free trail between Hayfield and New Mills for walkers, cyclists and horse riders. Passing through interesting and attractive countryside, visitors can appreciate the flora produced by the varying terrain. Before reaching the Torrs there is a spectacular gorge at the confluence of the rivers Sett and Goyt.

SHIPLEY PARK, ILKESTON
Route: M1, exit 26. A601 to Heanor then south-west on A608; the car park is signed. There is an unsurfaced car park from the A6007 Heanor-Ilkeston road. A charge is made for parking at weekends and Bank Holidays.

The Park, which will take many years to reach its full potential, aims to combine all the features of both a Country and Leisure

Park. Visitors will find a nature and woodland trail, a nature reserve and fishing facilities on Osborne's Pond and Adam's Pond for float fishing and on Mapperley Reservoir for fly fishing and ledgering. Anglers should hold the appropriate rod licence available from the Severn-Trent Water Authority and if possible be a member of the local fishing club. For day tickets, which are limited, application should be made to the Park Ranger.

At the present time sailing on Shipley lake is restricted to permit holders only (issued quarterly). Canoes and inflatable craft may use the lake at their own risk and day tickets, obtainable in advance from the Woodside Ranger Post, may be used on weekdays between 9.30 am and dusk. All those using the lake must provide life jackets. These facilities are being extended and details can be obtained from the Rangers. Model boating is permitted on the shallow northern lagoon area and a small portion adjacent to the main lake.

For horse riders and cyclists, bridleways and tracks are clearly marked. Please always ride with care as there may be children and dogs on the paths. Galloping is forbidden except in the designated area. Shipley Park Riding School offers tuition and hacking to visitors with or without their own horses. Telephone Mr Scott, Ilkeston (0602) 303673, for details.

For the young in heart a miniature railway operates on 1000 feet of landscaped track (weather permitting) on Sundays and Bank Holiday Mondays between 2.30 and 6.30 pm. Future amenities will include an 18 hole golf course, visitor centre, dairy farm and camping and caravan sites.

THE TISSINGTON TRAIL

The Trail lies along the route of the former Ashbourne to Buxton railway, beginning at Ashbourne at the southern end and continuing as far as Parsley Hay to the north. Access points by road are at Mapleton Lane, Ashbourne; Tissington; Alsop-le-Dale; Hartington, just west of the road; Parsley Hay; and Hurdlow. All points have parking and picnic facilities; Tissington, Hartington and Parsley Hay also have toilets. During the summer on Sundays and Bank Holiday Mondays an Information Centre is open in the old Signal Box in Hartington.

The development of the Trail began in January 1968 when rails and sleepers were removed from the disused line. The following year the ground was covered, rolled and seeded with grass and the derelict station properties demolished. The Trail routes are signposted and provide circular walks from each of the car parks. Walking routes are indicated by yellow markers, pony trekking routes by red markers, and where possible adjoining places of interest are indicated. Although routes are marked with directional signs, after leaving the Trail walkers must find their own way to their destinations.

WALKS BY THE RESERVOIRS

In the upper valley of the Derwent, north of Bamford, are three reservoirs, the Howden, the Derwent and the Ladybower. Walks here include:-

(1)   From the Derwent Dam to Derwent Edge.

(2)   From the head of the Howden Reservoir upstream to Slippery Stones. Note here the pack-horse bridge which was originally at Derwent. The Ladybower Reservoir, completed in 1945, submerged the villages of Derwent and Ashopton. For several years the spire of Derwent church rose above the surface of the water, until it was demolished during a drought in 1959, when the bridge was also moved to its present position.

(3)   Across the pack-horse bridge to Cranberry Clough and below Margery Hill, 1,793 feet.

(4)   From the bridge over the Westend river a long walk goes over the moors to Glossop, a shorter walk goes to Alport Castles.

10.   Sports and Hobbies

ANGLING

The rivers and reservoirs within Derbyshire are renowned for the splendid fishing they offer. However, *all* the waters within the Peak District National Park are under the private control of syndicates, clubs or riparian owners, and permission *must* first be obtained. The river Dove is noted for trout and grayling, and the rare rainbow trout are found in the river Wye near Buxton and the Derwent. The Manifold, Lathkill and Amber rivers, and the Longford and Bradford brooks are also well known for trout fishing. Guests at certain of the local hotels may fish in stretches of the trout streams at reasonable charges. These include the Isaac Walton Hotel near Ilam; The Crew and Cowper Arms Hotel, Longnor; the Cavendish Hotel, Baslow; the Peacock Hotel, Rowsley; the Rutland Arms, Bakewell and the Marquis of Granby Hotel at Bamford.

Coarse fishing is also popular and the rivers and reservoirs contain pike, dace and barbel. Nearly all the rivers are controlled by the Severn-Trent Water Authority which also holds the rights on the Ladybower, Lightwood, Ogston and Stanley Moor Reservoirs. Fly fishing only is permitted on the reservoirs and the season varies from either April or June to October. Details should be obtained from the Authority.

The North West Water Authority controls the rights on the Todd Brook,Whaley Bridge and Vale House Reservoirs. Many other lakes in parks or in private ownership can be fished on application to the owner.

Application for rod licences should be made to either The Severn-Trent Water Authority, Area Amenities Office, Meadow Lane, Nottingham, or the North-West Water Authority (Rivers Division), New Town House, Buttermarket Street, Warrington.

ARCHERY

This ancient sport has an enthusiastic following in Derbyshire. Meets are held throughout the county between April and October. Indoor facilities are enjoyed by the Alfreton Archers and the Rolls-Royce Bowmen. Field archery is practised on the grounds of the Derbyshire Club and the Derwent Bowmen. Seven other clubs have grounds of varying size. Tuition and 'Have a Go' sessions are arranged. On Sundays in summer the Derby club holds a number of shoots on the South Lawn of Kedleston Hall. For further details and information please contact the Association Secretary at 61, Wilmot Street, New Sawley, Long Eaton, Nottingham.

CANOEING

Although many of the rivers in the Peak District are suitable for canoeing, permission MUST be sought before entering the water. It is advisable to contact the River Adviser for the British Canoe Union, Mr. J. Bellhouse, at 12 Byron Road, West Bridgford, Nottingham, who will be able to give detailed information. A stamped addressed envelope would be appreciated.

CAVING

Caving is a very specialised hobby, and it is essential that those interested should join a recognised caving club. There are a number of clubs, within the county and details of these may be obtained by writing, enclosing a stamped addressed envelope, to the Derbyshire Caving Association, c/o 26 Musters Road, West Bridgford, Nottingham, NG2 7PL. It cannot be stressed too strongly that this is *not* a sport for the inexperienced. People who act irresponsibly bring danger not only to themselves but to their rescuers.

A short introduction to caving for beginners, led by an experienced caver, is available at Bagshaw Cavern, Bradwell, and courses are run from the Losehill Hall Study Centre and the White Hall Centre.

COUNTRY PURSUITS CENTRES

Hopton Cottage: Near Wirksworth. The self-catering cottage provides basic dormitory accommodation for up to 16 people, with a minimum age of 14. Visitors bring their own bed linen. Set at the top of the Hopton Incline on the High Peak Trail, visitors have the opportunity to study the trails described on page 59 and the Cromford Canal, page 22. Ornithologists and botanists will have ample material for field studies. Bookings can be made for weekends or week days, or a combination of up to 13 nights. Applications should be made to the County Planning Officer, Derbyshire County Council, County Offices, Matlock.

Edale Adventure Holidays: The Warren, Edale. A week in the summer or a winter weekend break are offered at this holiday centre. Visitors are encouraged to take part in various activities which are designed for both the novice or more proficient participant. Pony trekking, sailing, rock climbing, hill walking, orienteering and caving are included in the programme. For relaxation there is a heated swimming pool. Minimum age is 20, no upper limit! A special period is set aside for families.

Losehill Hall Study Centre: Peak Park Planning Board. This beautiful Victorian manor house is set in 27 acres of gardens and woodland in the centre of the National Park, half a mile east of Castleton.

An extensive programme is offered with both day and residential courses including National Park studies, archaeology, photography, rambling, ornithology, country crafts and painting. Activity holidays include tuition in sailing, riding, walking, cycling and caving. Accommodation for 60 people is provided in single or double rooms and families are welcome. Comfortable lounges, lecture rooms with a range of audio-visual equipment, a library and a shop are all to be found in the house. Enquiries should be made to the Principal at the Centre. A special service is offered to schools and youth groups.

The Wharf Shed Countryside Centre: The Centre is situated in an interesting old building associated with the Cromford Canal and High Peak Railway. The comfortable self-catering accommodation is in dormitory style, each containing 12 bunk beds. A classroom/laboratory allows students to carry out individual experiments associated with various field studies. Canoeing is available on the canal and there are opportunities for climbers and walkers. For further particulars apply to the Principal, Lea Green Sports Centre, Lea, Matlock.

White Hall Centre for Open Country Pursuits: Long Hill, Buxton. Weekend and longer courses are offered by the Centre in caving, canoeing, rock-climbing, sailing, hill walking and mountaineering. Minimum age is 15 — no maximum! All equipment and special clothing is included in the course fee which also covers tuition by qualified instructors and accommodation. Full details are obtainable from the Principal.

CYCLING

The Cyclists' Touring Club is a national organisation catering for every kind of cyclist. The Derby District Association of the C.T.C. was founded in 1924 and provides a full and varied programme of cycling and social activities. The Tour of the Peak cycle race takes place in September. Cycles are available for hire on the High Peak Trail from Parsley Hay and Middleton Top, and for the Tissington Trail at Ashbourne. Similar facilities are available at Monsal Head, tel. Great Longstone 505, and for the Upper Derwent Valley, tel. Bakewell 2881.

GLIDING

The Derbyshire and Lancashire Gliding Club, Great Hucklow, Near Buxton.

The airfield is situated on a small plateau overlooking the valleys of Eyam, Bradwell and Hope. Once a medieval farm, the clubhouse has been extensively modernised and is complete with sleeping accommodation, dining room and an old world bar. The large hanger can house twelve fully-rigged aircraft. There are three two-seater gliders used for training, two single-seaters for early solo soaring and cross-country flights and a more advanced sailplane for experienced pilots. Many privately owned gliders are kept on the site. A series of weekly courses are run throughout the summer for members of the public. Pupils acquire the skills required in ground-work and glider handling as well as the flying itself. As flying is dependant on weather it is advisable to bring plenty of warm clothing, an anorak and heavy shoes. Pillowcases and sheets or a sleeping bag are required for residential courses.

HANG GLIDING
The Peak District Flight Training School, Upper Hulme, Leek.

The school is conveniently positioned at the Roaches crags which mark the foot of the Pennines. After a period of simulator training, pupils progress to gentle slopes, affording maximum safety. They are only allowed to graduate to bigger slopes when the necessary skills have been acquired. Light windproof clothing is advised, strong walking shoes — to get you back to base, and a pair of good leather gloves. Helmets are provided by the school to ensure they reach the required safety standards. A pilot may not fly unless covered by 3rd party insurance to a value accepted by the British Hang Gliding Association.

RAMBLING
Gentle walks or rambles are enjoyed by many through the beautiful scenery of the Derbyshire dales, and paths are well marked especially within the National Park. For rambling on the moors walking boots and waterproof clothing are essential, plus warm brightly coloured garments in order that anyone in difficulties may easily be seen by rescuers. An ordnance survey map, a compass, a whistle and enough food to last a day should always be carried. Check local weather conditions beforehand, as these may change very quickly, and never leave without telling someone of your intended route and expected time of return, remembering to inform them when you are safely back.

Discovery Trails, for which booking is essential, are organised by the Peak Park Planning Board for individuals and families from April to mid-October. Strong shoes and warm and waterproof clothing are advised. The average time allowed is 3 hours. Trails depart from various centres and cover a wide and varied range of subjects. Further details and bookings from Bakewell (062 981) 2881, Ext. 54, between 8.45 am and 5 pm weekdays only.

Guided walks of general interest and about two hours' duration, for which no booking is required, take place each Sunday from the middle of June to the end of September at 2 pm. Venues are the car parks at Bakewell and Edale. Additional walks start at 11am from the last Sunday in July at Castleton and Hartington. A small charge is made.

Rambling weekends and guided walks are organised at Losehill Hall Study Centre and details may be obtained from the Principal.

RIDING AND PONY TREKKING

Ashbourne: Callow Riding Stables, Mapleton Road. Mrs. C. Ferry. Riding tuition for children and adults. Trekking and hacking in lovely countryside.

Darley Dale: The Darley School of Equitation, Red House Stables. Miss Caroline Dale. Qualified tuition and hacking by the hour or day. Children's six day holiday, riding and having fun with horses and ponies.

Derby: Markeaton Riding Centre, Markeaton Lane. Mrs. V. Pollard. Riding instruction for both adults and children. Large indoor school. Children taken for riding holidays.

Edale. Ladybooth Riding and Trekking Centre. R.A. Atkin (Member of the English Riding (Holiday) and Trekking Association). Trekking and riding in the Edale and Hope Valleys. Riding holidays arranged in conjunction with the Youth Hostels Association.

Quarnford: Thick Withins Riding and Trekking Centre, near Buxton. Miss Abbott. One to three day instructional courses. Trekking all year in the Dove and Manifold valleys. Families and small groups welcome.

Stanley: Whitehouse Farm Riding School, Morley Lane. Miss J.M. Brassington. A small school specialising in instruction for children. Weekly courses during the summer.

Although only a few of the many riding centres in Derbyshire, those mentioned above are included in the British Horse Society's list of 'Where to Ride'.

ROCK CLIMBING

The Peak District contains a wide variety of climbs both on millstone grit and on limestone. The millstone grit affords easier climbs, including the gorge below Kinder Downfall and Yellowslacks brook on Bleaklow. The limestone terrain is higher and the climbs more difficult. More specialised equipment is needed for these climbs which include Chee Dale and Monsal Dale. There are a number of local clubs whose object is to bring together people who are interested in all the many aspects of mountaineering. Eight day mountaineering courses are run at the White Hall Country Pursuits Centre.

SAILING

Sailing is popular on the numerous reservoirs throughout the county. Although in most cases restricted to members of affiliated clubs, visitors may often become temporary members and enjoy the facilities offered. Application should be made to the local secretaries. See also Shipley Lake page 64.

A coach and four at Darley School of Equitation

SHOOTING

The Yeaveley Shooting Grounds, Church Farm, Yeaveley, near Ashbourne, have facilities for clay pigeon shooting, with tuition and practice on such birds as pheasants, driven grouse, partridge and snipe, etc., all under realistic conditions. Beginners and visitors are welcomed and there are guns on loan for their use. Shoots, open to anyone, are held on the last Sunday in each month. The Muzzle Loader Shoots have the most spectator appeal as many competitors take part in period costume.

STAGE COACH DRIVING

Red House Stables, Darley Dale.

The romantic era of the stage coach is re-enacted in Darley Dale. From here a trip can be taken to Chatsworth Park, Bakewell and Haddon Hall, stopping at a coaching inn for lunch. For the more adventurous, a three day tour can be undertaken. Tuition is given in driving singles, pairs, tandem and four-in-hand, either by the hour or day. Lectures and demonstrations are arranged for groups and schools who also have the opportunity to see the extensive carriage collection. All the carriages are authentic and include two stage coaches used on the London - Edinburgh and Leeds - Birmingham runs, a western covered wagon, a landau, brougham and hansom cab, in addition to 'owner driven' phaetons and a display of commercial and farm vehicles. All enquiries should be made to Mrs. Caroline Dale at the Stables. Telephone Darley Dale (062 983) 3583.

11. Customs

ALPORT CASTLE WOODLANDS LOVE FEAST
Alport farm is along a track. 1½ miles north of the A57 Sheffield to Manchester road, approximately 5 miles west of the junction with the A6013.

The Love Feast is a religious ceremony dating back to 1662 when Methodist clergy were ejected from their livings and hounded to this remote Derbyshire farm, following the Act of Uniformity, and is always held on the first Sunday in July. The barn in which the meeting takes place is believed to be the original one; the congregation all take part, telling of their Christian experiences, leading in prayer, reading from the Scriptures and suggesting hymns to be sung. At one point in the proceedings baskets containing portions of plum cake are passed round together with two 'Loving Cups' of water.

ASHBOURNE SHROVETIDE FOOTBALL MATCH
The game was first thought to have been introduced into England in the time of Henry II and to Ashbourne in the reign of Elizabeth I. Once played in many Midland towns and as far north as Durham, it is in Ashbourne that it retains much of its old character. The game is played between two teams consisting of both men and women who are eligible only by birthright, and are known as "The Up'ards" and "The Down'ards" depending upon which side of Henmore Brook they live. Always made in Ashbourne, the ball is also traditional. The leather used is first of all soaked for many hours to soften it and then cut into panels which are sewn together with a waxed thread; it is stuffed tightly with fine cork dust and finally sewn up. Two balls, the first to be thrown up on either day, Shrove Tuesday or Ash Wednesday, are by tradition painted.

The person throwing up the ball is always entertained to lunch at the Green Man Hotel. Afterwards he takes the ball and walks to Shaw Croft, a small field in the centre of the town, where he is hoisted on the shoulders of two men and appeals to the players for sporting play. "Auld Lang Syne" and "God Save the Queen" are then sung and the ball "thrown up". In 1928 the late Duke of Windsor, then the Prince of Wales, threw up the ball and since this time the game has been known as "The Royal Shrovetide Football".

The game is a "free for all" and those playing wear old clothes and stout shoes. The goal posts are three miles apart — the Down'ards must score by touching the wall where a mill wheel used to be at Clifton; the Up'ards must score at Sturston Mill. The person scoring a goal is allowed to keep the ball. After the ball has been "thrown" it may be kicked, picked up or carried — there is usually some water play when the ball goes into the river Henmore or the Fish Pond. The sentiments of the game are summed up in the last two lines of a local song: —

It's a good old game, deny it who can,
That tries the pluck of an Englishman.

CASTLETON: ROYAL OAK APPLE DAY
May 29th commemorates the day in 1660 when Charles II landed at Dover and was restored to the throne. Annually on that date in Castleton, a man representing the king and wearing a large garland of flowers and leaves which almost envelop his head and shoulders rides through the streets of the town on horse back, "Queen Catherine" riding beside him. They are accompanied by a band and Morris dancers to the market square where a maypole is pleated. At dusk the great garland is hoisted to the top of the church tower. Here it remains until it has withered and rotted away. The ceremony has been carried out for the last 300 years. (See also pages 9 and 39 for places of interest in the area).

WAKES
Wakes are held throughout northern England, and in Derbyshire many towns and villages observe this ancient custom. A "Wake" means to "keep vigil" and takes place on the anniversary of the patron saint of a parish church, the origins of which may be Anglo-Saxon. In the middle ages, on the eve of the anniversary, the floor of the church would be strewn with rushes and flowers; boughs were used to decorate the pulpit and altar. Parishioners from neighbouring villages were accommodated in tents in the churchyard and they all attended the service of dedication. The following day was observed as a holiday and soon evolved into country fairs. Wakes are still held at Kirk Ireton, Hope, Eyam, Tideswell, and Winster, although many carnival weeks are held in other parishes in connection with well-dressing ceremonies. (see below, Well-Dressings).

WELL-DRESSING
The origins of well-dressing can almost certainly be traced back to the stone age when pagans offered sacrifice to propitiate the water gods; it may also be connected with the Druid festival of Blessing the Streams, when flowers and garlands were cast upon the water. Evidence of Neolithic and Druid remains are to be found throughout Derbyshire, which may be why this is a typical custom in the county. As Christianity spread the tradition was adapted by the church as a thanksgiving for water and the wells were dressed accordingly.

Today the dressings are made up on strong wooden boards or frames, covered in clay which is held in place by hundreds of nails. Pre-prepared pictures, usually with Biblical backgrounds, are pricked out in the clay with an awl and built up with natural materials — alder cones, maize, berries, moss, small vegetables, flowers and petals. Tradition dictates the materials used in each town or village and the exact method of preparation. Each dressing will take a team of six or more people about three days to make, and can last for up to a week, depending on the weather.

At *Tissington* the earliest known tradition of well-dressing is carried out, and dates either from the time when the village escaped a plague in 1348/9, attributed to the purity of the water, or from 1615 when, during a severe drought, the wells never ran dry; since that time the annual Ascension Day thanksgiving has continued. Five wells are dressed, Hall Well, Town Well, Hand's Well, Yew Tree Well and Coffin Well. After a service in the church a procession, led by the clergy and choir, visit each well in turn.

Other well-dressings are as follows:

Ashford-in-the-Water: On A6020 near Bakewell. The custom lapsed for some years prior to 1945 when it was re-introduced. Held on Trinity Sunday, many people are attracted to the service and procession.

Barlow: North-west of Chesterfield on B6051, held on the Wednesday after the 2nd Sunday in August. Three wells are blessed and the screens are dressed in situ with whole flowers.

Bonsall: Near Matlock off A5012. The ceremony takes place on the Sunday after the Patronal Festival, July 25th, beginning in the church with an act of thanksgiving for water and all the benefits it brings. A procession then tours the sites of the well-screens and a hymn relevant to the theme adopted is sung.

Bradwell: On B6049 south of the A625 Sheffield road. During the first week of August the ceremonies take place, followed as in many places with a week of carnival events and special activities.

Buxton: Well-dressing dates from 1840 when water was first piped into the town's fountain in higher Buxton. By 1863 it is known that St. Anne's Well was also being dressed and it is these two wells that are blessed on the Wednesday of the second week in July.

Edlaston and Wyaston: On unclassified road three miles south of Ashbourne off A515. Edlaston well was given to the village in 1869 and that at Wyaston in 1871. The blessings take place jointly during early July.

Etwall: On A516 south-west of Derby. The stream or spring of Eta, now known as Town Well and housed to the west of the church, was probably the "Eta waella" from which the name of the town was derived. The well-dressing takes place at Whitsun.

Eyam: On B6251 north of Bakewell celebrates its well-dressing on the last Saturday in August at various wells in the village. Mompesson's well, used during the time of the plague, is not blessed as it is about a mile outside the village. (See also page 32).

Hope: On A625 Sheffield road. Three tableaux are blessed on the Saturday nearest to the 29th June. The choir and clergy process from well to well; a hymn is sung to the accompaniment of a brass band and a prayer is offered.

Litton: South off A623 east of Buxton. The well blessing service is held in the afternoon of the Sunday nearest to 24th June.

Pilsley: On unclassified road west of A6023 north of Bakewell. The ancient custom was revived in 1967 and takes place a few days prior to the third Saturday in July. The original well being inaccessible the dressing takes place on the village green.

Rowsley: On A6 north of Matlock. The well, opposite the Peacock Hotel, is dressed for the last week-end in June and is blessed at an open-air service on the

74

Bradwell Well Screen

Sunday at 10.30 am. A Flower Festival is held in St. Katherine's Church on the same date.

Stoney Middleton: On A623 north of Bakewell. The thermal baths near the church are of ancient origin. The wells are dressed on the Saturday before the first Monday in August.

Tideswell: On B6049 east of Buxton. Well-dressing is held on June 24th at the site of the village well in Fountain Square with an open air service of thanksgiving at 3 pm.

Wirksworth: On B5023 south of Matlock. The town has dressed the wells since 1827, probably earlier, this date marking the provision of piped water. The screens are erected on the spots where standpipes were placed at that time, and are blessed on the Spring Bank Holiday weekend.

Wormhill: On unclassified road off B6049 east of Buxton. Prior to 1891 well-dressing was known to have taken place at Wormhill Springs. The blessing now takes place at the Brindley Memorial Well-head on the Saturday of the late Summer Bank Holiday.

Youlgreave: On B5056 south of Bakewell. The ceremony of blessing the wells takes place on the Saturday nearest to the 24th June; five wells or taps, dating from 1829 when the local Water Board was inaugurated, are dressed.

The churches of Bakewell, Eyam, Tideswell, Tissington, Worksworth and Youlgreave are described on pages 29 to 37.

12.   Events

WE would like to thank all those who have supplied information for this chapter. It will be appreciated that exact dates and venues can not always be given, and in these instances we would ask readers to refer to the local press. The following list of addresses where further information can be obtained may be found useful: —

DERBYSHIRE COUNTY COUNCIL, County Planning Department, County Offices, Matlock.

PEAK DISTRICT NATIONAL PARK.
Applications for written information should be made to: Aldern House, Baslow Road, Bakewell.
Information Centres: Castleton and Edale.

ENGLISH TOURIST BOARD INFORMATION CENTRES.

Alfreton:	Public Library, Severn Square.
Ashbourne:	13, Market Place.
Bolsover:	Library, Church Street.
Chesterfield:	Library, Corporation Street.
Derby:	Reference Department, Central Library.
Ilkeston:	Public Library, Market Place.
Long Eaton:	Central Library, Tamworth Road.
Matlock Bath:	Matlock Bath Pavilion.

Information on Youth Hostels and caravan sites, and lists of landowners and farmers who have indicated they are willing to take occasional campers are available from the Peak District National Park Centre at Bakewell.

AGRICULTURAL SHOWS are held throughout the county and include the Derbyshire County Show in Elvaston Country Park during May; the Midland Counties Show at Cromford Meadows in June; the Ashby-de-la-Zouch and District Show at Calke Park, Ticknell, in July; the Ashbourne Show on the third Saturday in August and also during the month the Bakewell and Belper Shows. Early in September a Country Fair is held at Chatsworth.

FARM OPEN DAYS
Each year the County Council arranges for a few Derbyshire farms to hold open days. For further information telephone Matlock (0629) 3411, ext. 7164.

MATLOCK BATH ILLUMINATIONS
Venetian Nights, band concerts and fireworks from mid-August to mid-October.

MORRIS DANCERS
During the summer members of the Chapel, Chesterfield and Stafford Morris Men give displays at various towns and villages throughout the county.

PLOUGHING MATCHES are held during October at Brailsford and West Hallam.

SHEEP-DOG TRIALS
Major contests take place at Bamfield in May. During August trials are held at Hope, Ilam and Lyme Park and in September at Longshaw and Hayfield.

STOCK AND BANGER CAR RACING meetings are held regularly from April to October at the High Edge Raceway, Buxton.

THEATRES IN DERBYSHIRE AND THE PEAK

Buxton: Playhouse Theatre.
Opera House - opened 1979.

Derby: Assembly Rooms.
Derby Playhouse.
also 'The Studio', a small intimate theatre situated beneath the Playhouse.

Chesterfield: The Civic Theatre.

Matlock: The Pavilion.

THREE DAY EVENTS are held at Chatsworth Park in October and Locko Park during August.

Index

79